C

Introduction

Food Finder

Our choice:

INTRODUCTION

Time for Food guides are designed to help you find interesting and enjoyable places to eat in the world's main tourist destinations. Each guide divides the destination into eight areas. Each area has a map, followed by a selection of the restaurants, cafés, bars, pubs and food markets in that area. The aim is to cover the whole spectrum of food establishments, from gourmet temples to humble cafés, plus good food shops or delicatessens where you can buy picnic ingredients or food to cook yourself.

If you are looking for a particular restaurant, regardless of its location, or a particular type of cuisine, you can turn to the Food Finder, starting on page 4. This lists all the establishments reviewed in this guide by name (in alphabetical order) and then by cuisine type.

PRICES

Unlike some guides, we have not wasted space telling you how bad a restaurant is – bad or poor-value restaurants simply do not make it into the guide. Many other guides ask restaurants to pay for their entries, or expect the restaurant to advertise in return for a listing. We do neither of these things: the restaurants and cafés featured here simply represent a selection of places that the author has sampled and enjoyed.

If there is one consistent criterion for inclusion in the guide, it is good

▲ Piazzale Michelangiolo

value. Good value does not, of course, mean cheap necessarily. Food lovers know the difference between a restaurant where the high prices are fully justified by the quality of the ingredients and the excellence of the cooking and presentation of the food, and meretricious establishments where high prices are merely the result of pretentious attitudes.

Some of the restaurants featured here are undeniably expensive if you consume caviar and champagne, but even haute cuisine establishments offer set-price menus (especially at lunchtime) allowing budget diners to enjoy dishes created by top chefs and every bit as good as those on the regular menu. At the same time, some of the eating places listed here might not make it into more conventional food guides, because they are relatively humble cafés or takeaways. Some are deliberately oriented towards tourists, but there is nothing wrong in that: what some guides dismiss as 'tourist traps' may be deservedly popular for providing choice and good value.

FEEDBACK

You may or may not agree with the author's choice – in either case we would like to know about your experiences. Any feedback you give us and any recommendations you make will be followed up, so that you can look forward to seeing your restaurant suggestions in print in the next edition.

Feedback forms have been included at the back of the book and you can e-mail us with comments by writing to: *timeforfood@thomascook.com*. No food guide can keep pace with the changing restaurant scene, as chefs move on, establishments open or close, and menus, opening hours or credit card details change. Let us know what you like or do not like about the restaurants featured here. Tell us if you discover shops, pubs, cafés, bars, restaurants or markets that

you think should go in the guide. Let us know if you discover changes – say to telephone numbers or opening times.

Symbols used in this guide

VISA	Visa accepted
🅾	Diners Club accepted
MasterCard	MasterCard accepted
🍴	Restaurant
🍷	Bar, café or pub
🧺	Shop, market or picnic site
✆	Telephone
🚉	Transport
❷	Numbered red circles relate to the maps at the start of the section

The price indications used in this guide have the following meanings:

❻	budget level
❻❻	typical/average for the destination
❻❻❻	up-market

Oltrarno

This quiet neighbourhood of picturesque streets and squares on the embankment of the River Arno is dotted with homely trattorias and traditional wine bars. If you're in the area be sure to visit the exquisite hillside church of San Miniato al Monte, founded in 1018.

[Map of Oltrarno area showing streets including Borgo d.Stella, V. S. Monaca, V. Maffia, V. S. Spirito, V. de' Serragli, V. S. Agostino, Pza S. Spirito, Tegolaio, Borgo, V. Maggio, V. Toscanelli, V. delle Caldaie, V. Guicciardini, V. S. Maria, V. Romana, Giardino Bòboli, with scale bars showing 0–250 metres and 0–250 yards]

OLTRARNO
Restaurants

Alfredo sull' Arno ①

V. de' Bardi 46r

☎ 055 283808

🚌 Bus D

Open: Mon–Sat 1200–1430, 1700–2230

Reservations unnecessary

All credit cards accepted

Tuscan-Italian

€€

Restaurant geared mainly for tourists with a small terrace overlooking the Arno and the Ponte Vecchio. Choice of menus including à la carte and 'chef's recommendation'.

Il Barone di Porta Romana ②

V. Romana 123r

☎ 055 220585

🚌 Buses 11, 36 and 37

Open: Mon–Sat 1900–2300

Reservations recommended

All credit cards accepted

Tuscan-International

€€

The antique furnishings and candlelit tables give this attractive restaurant a romantic ambience.

The food is nothing special – most guests are more interested in the appetisers and foreign wines. The entertainment has a Spanish flavour with a flamenco show most nights and a 'Spanish evening' on Saturdays.

Bibò ③

Pza S. Felicita 6r

☎ 055 2398554

🚌 Bus D

Open: daily 1200–1430, 1900–2230

Reservations unnecessary

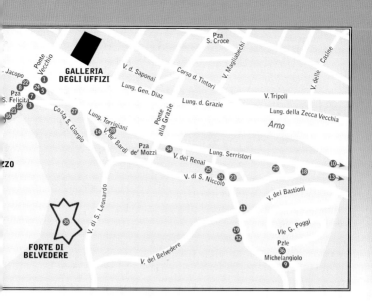

▲ Bibò

Trattoria Bordino

CHIUSO LA DOMENICA

via stracciatella, 9 R
50125 firenze

tel. 055/213048

All credit cards accepted

Tuscan

€€

Located in a quiet square off the busy Via Guicciardini, this restaurant by the Ponte Vecchio offers typical Florentine cooking. There's a fixed price, three-course menu.

Boboli 4

V. Romana 45r

✆ 055 2336401

🚌 Buses 11, 36 and 37

Open: Thu–Tue 1100–1500, 1900–2400

Reservations unnecessary

Tuscan

€-€€

Boboli is a homely trattoria located just beyond the Pitti Palace on the Porta Romana road. The speciality of the house is *bistecca alla fiorentina*, but you'll also find grilled pork cutlet and veal escalope on the menu, as well as a tasty spaghetti with lobster sauce. Usual range of Tuscan wines.

Bordino 5

V. Stracciatella 9r

✆ 055 213048

🚌 Bus D

Open: Mon–Sat 1200–1430, 1930–2230

Reservations unnecessary

All credit cards accepted

Tuscan-Italian

€€

Located in a quiet square off Via Guicciardini, this pleasant trattoria has an intimate feel with cellar-like brick walls and a vaulted ceiling. Save room for the mouth-watering desserts.

Il Caffè 6

Pza Pitti 9

✆ 055 2396241

🚌 Bus D

Open: daily 1100–0200, lunch 1200–1600

Reservations unnecessary

No credit cards accepted

Tuscan

€

The ideal spot for lunch after a heavy-duty tour of the Palazzo Pitti opposite. There are two set menus: an *antipasto* with a choice of *primi piatti*, or a modest three-course option. Service is prompt and courteous. Entertainment after dark in the form of live music (including jazz) attracts a mainly young Italian crowd, dropping in for cocktails or Irish coffee (a speciality of the house).

Celestino 7

Pza S. Felicita 4r

✆ 055 2396574

🚌 Bus D

Open: Mon–Sat 1200–1430, 1930–2230

Reservations unnecessary

All credit cards accepted

Tuscan

€€

Just 30m from the Ponte Vecchio, Celestino is a roomy establishment, somewhat lacking in atmosphere, but with outside dining in the summer. There's a fixed price menu.

La Galleria 8

V. Guicciardini 48r

✆ 055 218545

🚌 Bus D

Open: Tue–Sun 1300–1500, 1815–2215

Reservations unnecessary

All credit cards accepted

Italian

€€

A modern restaurant in La Galleria shopping precinct off the main street, with a good line in pizzas as well as a choice of *secondi*. There's a menu of the day and a fixed price menu.

Loggia 9

Pzle Michelangiolo 1

✆ 055 234832

🚌 Buses 12 and 13

Open: Thu–Tue 1000–2300

Patronised as much for its views of the city as for its classic Italian cuisine, Loggia was denounced by the architect of the *piazzale*, Giuseppe Poggi, who had intended it to house plaster casts of works by Michelangelo; but that was in 1875!

L'Orologio 🔟

V. Giam Paolo Orsini 86r

✆ 055 6811729

🚌 Buses 8, 12, 13, 23, 33, 80 and D

Open: Mon–Sat 1200–1500, 1930–2330, closed Sat pm

Reservations recommended

All credit cards accepted

Tuscan-Italian

€€

'The Clock' is a welcoming trattoria, serving such standards as *ribollita*, *zuppa di faro* (wheat and bean soup), *ragù* (ragout), risotto and *ossobuco* (stew made with knuckle of veal in tomato sauce), *trippa alla fiorentina* (tripe stewed with tomatoes, onion, carrot, parmesan and white wine) and *francesina* (boiled beef and carrots).

Osteria Antica Mescita 11️⃣

V. S. Niccolò 60r

✆ 055 2342836

🚌 Buses 12, 13, 23 and D

Open: Mon–Sat 1000–2300

Reservations recommended

No credit cards accepted

Tuscan

€

A traditional wine shop or *mescita*, this cosy little place, near the church of San Niccolò Oltrarno, does duty as both restaurant and wine bar. The plain Tuscan dishes – *pappa al pomodoro* recommended as a starter – are ideally accompanied by a decent bottle of Chianti Classico; or you might go for the bargain 'English roast beef.'

Small, honest and friendly.

La Sagrestia 12️⃣

V. Guicciardini 27r

✆ 055 210003

🚌 Bus D

Open: Tue–Sun 1200–1500, 1830–2230

Reservations recommended

All credit cards accepted

Tuscan-Italian

€€

Smart restaurant in the Oltrarno district, conveniently situated between the Ponte Vecchio and the Pitti Palace. Wood-panelled walls and copies of classical paintings by the likes of Botticelli in the recesses give the place a warm, refined feel. The pleasingly presented *secondi* include entrecôte with gorgonzola, tenderloin with peppers and mustard sauce, and roast chicken, while for starters you could try the pasta with crab, cooked in a spicy tomato sauce.

▲ Loggia

OLTRARNO
Bars, cafés and pubs

Bagel House 13

V. dei Bastioni 47	
✆ 055 2480999	
🚌 Buses 12 and 13	
Open: Tue–Fri 1100–1930, Sat 1100–1330, 1530–1930, Sun 1100–0100	
€	

Not only bagels, but American cookies, cheesecake and Mom's apple pie. Small and busy, it attracts a predominantly student crowd. Phone orders accepted.

Bar Arno 14

V. de' Bardi 41	
✆ None available	
🚌 Bus D	
Open: daily 0800–2000	
€	

Snack bar with counter service and limited seating, full of people on the go. The mainstay foodwise is pizza, but there's also a set menu.

Bar Pitti 15

Pza Pitti 20	
✆ None available	
🚌 Bus D	
Open: daily 0800–2400	
€	

This lozenge-shaped bar with a *sala da tè* (tearoom) attracts a genteel, predominantly youthful clientele. Some outside seating.

Il Birrocchio 16

V. Guicciardini 39	
✆ None available	
🚌 Bus D	
Open: daily 0800–2000	
€	

Small, neighbourhood bar specialising in bottled beers (local and imported). You'll also find a large choice of pizzas and sandwiches.

Caffè Bellini 17

Pza Pitti 6r	
✆ None available	
🚌 Bus D	
Open: daily 0800–2000	
€	

Founded in 1895, this thoroughly respectable establishment opposite the Pitti Palace offers the usual mix of bread rolls, cakes, pastries, salami and wines, as well as coffee.

Caffè La Torre 18

Lung. Cellini 65r	
✆ 055 680643	
🚌 Buses 12, 13, 23 and D	
Open: daily 0830–0400	
€€	

One of the hottest spots in town, not least because of its long opening hours and its location beneath the ramparts of Piazzale Michelangiolo. In the mornings it's a popular

breakfast spot, offering brioches, muesli, corn flakes, pancakes with marmalade and English breakfasts. At other times of the day and night you can choose from fish dishes, pancakes, *primi* and salads, or sip an aperitif to the accompaniment of live music, predominantly jazz and Latin but with some pop.

L'Enoteca Fuori Porta 19

V. del Monte alle Croci 10r	
✆ 055 2342483	
🚌 Buses 12 and 13	
Open: Mon–Sat	
€€	

The 'Wine Bar Outside the Gates' can be found on the hilly approaches to the exquisite church of San Miniato al Monte and there's outside seating to enjoy the view. The food – mainly sandwiches, cheeses and appetisers – is very good and the selection of wines even better (at least 40 varieties available and sold by the glass).

Hostaria del Bricco 20

V. S. Niccolò 8r	
✆ 055 2345037	
🚌 Buses 12, 13, 23 and D	
Open: Tue–Sun 0930–1530	
€€	

A neighbourhood wine bar open for lunch, when it serves a limited selection of traditional Tuscan dishes.

Pinot

V. Guicciardini 16
✆ None available
🚍 Bus D
Open: daily 0800–2300
€

Local bar mainly with standing room selling sandwiches as well as the usual range of alcoholic and non-alcoholic drinks.

Ponte Vecchio

Ponte Vecchio 57r
✆ 055 210051
🚍 Bus D
Open: daily 0700–2300
€

A pity the outside tables aren't facing the bridge; nevertheless this is a pleasant sandwich bar with a great location for sightseers. Brisk efficient service. The main attraction is the ice cream, but pizza slices are also available.

Il Rifrullo ㉓

V. S. Niccolò 55r
✆ 055 2342621
🚍 Buses 12, 13, 23 and D
Open: daily 0800–0100
€

Beneath the walls of the church of San Niccolò, this modern bar is open for snack lunches, but doesn't really take off until evenings when the cocktail crowd arrives. Draught beers as well as wines are available, also sandwiches. Pleasant garden and plenty of room.

Le Volp E L'Uva ㉔

Pza dei Rossi
✆ 055 2398132
🚍 Bus D
Open: Mon–Sat 1000–2000
€€

'The Fox and Grapes' is a real find. Conveniently located behind the Ponte Vecchio, it offers an excellent choice of Chianti and other Tuscan wines, as well as a Cabernet Sauvignon from New Zealand and a French sparkling wine from the Loire (Vouvray Haigle d'Or Pagnatowski). The food on offer mainly consists of *antipasti* – sausage, cheeses, pâté (smoked swordfish), and so on.

Zoe ㉕

V. dei Renai 24
✆ 055 243111
🚍 Buses 12, 13, 23 and D
Open: Mon–Sat 0700–0100
€

Tucked away behind Piazza Niccolò Demidoff, this small modern bar with steel chairs and blue painted tables is calculated to appeal to trendy Florentines and visitors alike.

▲ Piazza Pitti

OLTRARNO
Shops, markets and picnic sites

Bakeries, confectioners and pasta shops

Il Fornaio 26

V. Guicciardini 3

 Bus D

Open: daily 0730–1930

Excellent stand-by for a light lunch (or picnic) if you're in the Ponte Vecchio area. Apart from a choice of bread rolls and toasts, there are spinach-filled pastries, Florentine biscuits, *torta semolina* (semolina cake), *pan frutto* (raisin bread), *strudel* and *torta di mele crostate* (apple tart).

Maioli 27

V. de' Bardi 71

 Bus D

Open: daily 0800–2000

Irresistible to anyone with a sweet tooth, the mouth-watering cakes and pastries on sale here include *bomboloni caldi* (hot doughnuts), carrot cake, chocolate cake and *cantuccini* (almond biscuits). Fast food in the form of pasta and hamburgers is also available at lunchtime.

Delicatessens and grocers

Alimentari 28

V. de' Bardi 61

 Bus D

Open: Mon–Sat 0600–2000, closed Wed pm

Grocery store, well-stocked with fruit and vegetables, preserves, wines, and so on.

Mokkarico 29

V. Romana 54

 Buses 11, 36 and 37

Open: daily 0700–1300, 1600–2000

This small *latteria* (implies fresh milk on sale) and grocery shop also sells a range of sandwiches and is useful for stocking up with picnic fare en route to the Arno embankment (*see page 15*).

Spar 30

V. Romana 50

 Buses 11, 36 and 37

Open: daily 0800–2000

Local branch of a supermarket chain with Tuscan wine specialities including Vin Santo and Chianti Classico; they also sell a highly drinkable Verrazano.

Ice cream

Frilli (Gelateria-latteria) 31

V. S. Miniato 5r

 Buses 12 and 13

Open: daily 0800–2200

The best ice-cream parlour this side of the river, Frilli also sells wines and imported beers.

Wine and oils

L'Enoteca Fuori Porta 32

V. del Monte alle Croci 10r

 Buses 12 and 13

Open: Mon–Sat 1100–2230

Wide range of wines and spirits for sale in this shop next door to the bar (*see page 12*).

Gola e Cantina 33

Pza Pitti 16

 Bus D

Open: daily 1000–1330, 1430–1930

A well-known *enoteca* with an excellent choice of Chianti Classico ranges – Fontodi, Rampolla, and so on – as well as French wines. It also sells local produce including sun-dried tomatoes and *tartufata nera* (black truffles), oils, jams, marmalades and a wonderful array of chocolates.

Picnic sites

Embankment gardens 34

 Buses 12, 13, 23, C and D

There are a couple of pleasant picnic spots, with shade, overlooking the Arno. In front of the Lutheran Church of **Santa Lucia dei Magnoli** are some benches where parents with young children come to feed the pigeons. A more attractive spot, with fewer parked cars, lies further along the embankment (Lungarno Serristori) at **Piazza Niccolò Demidoff** – the statue commemorates the noted Russian philanthropist who lived in Florence in the early 19th century.

Forte di Belvedere 35

🚌 Buses 12 and 13

Built by the Medici in 1590 as a potent symbol of Florentine supremacy, the fortress and adjoining city walls still dominate the south bank of the Arno and now provide the perfect setting for a picnic. There are wonderful views of the city and the surrounding countryside. and after lunch you can tour the ramparts before visiting the art exhibitions sometimes held in the *palazzina* and grounds.

Piazzale Michelangiolo 36

🚌 Buses 12 and 13

The *piazzale* was constructed in 1875, specifically with the growing tourist trade in mind, and has been on most itineraries ever since. You'll be hard pressed to find a more edifying picnic spot in Florence, as here you're surrounded by imposing copies of Michelangelo's sculptures, not to mention the local artists inspired by the panoramic views of the city. If you haven't brought your lunch with you, there's a small café-restaurant in the *loggia* at the back of the square (*see page 10*). After lunch, you could visit the beautiful church of **San Miniato al Monte** on the hill above, which boasts some wonderful medieval frescos and mosaics.

▲ Piazzale Michelangiolo

Business restaurants

Dining to impress

It's hardly surprising that Florence is a favourite destination for international conferences and business forums, with most of the leading hotels offering special business lunches and menus.

• **Alfredo** *Vle Don Giovanni Minzoni 3r; ✆ 055 578291;* 🖀 *buses 1 and 7; open: daily 1200–1430, 1900–2300; reservations essential; all credit cards accepted; Tuscan;* ❷❸. This small restaurant is perfect for that one-on-one dinner where you're getting to know a client or finalising the details of that elusive deal. The atmosphere is informal without being casual and the husband and wife team of Mario and Lucia Tosi strive to surprise. The smoked goose breast with salad works well as an appetiser, then try the traditional *tagliatta di manzo con rucola*

(beef slices with *rucola*). If you're a fish lover, keep your fingers crossed that the *orata agli agrumi* (sea bream with citrus fruits) is available. Save room for baked chocolate mousse served with mint ice cream.

• **Caffè Concerto** *Lung. Cristoforo Colombo 7; ✆ 055 677377;* 🖀 *buses 31 and 32; open: Mon–Sat; reservations recommended; all credit cards accepted; Tuscan;* ❶❷❸. The location is the Arno embankment, with views of the river from the veranda. Caffè Concerto is steadily growing in popularity. This is largely down to Gabriele Tachini's inventive way with traditional Tuscan cuisine – he's been fine tuning the menu now for more than 20 years. The list changes every month but recent offerings have included macaroni with cuttlefish or spelt with turnip soup, followed by fried pigeon marinated in a white wine sauce, or stew made with ass meat.

• **I due G** *V. Cennini 6r; ✆ 055 218623;* 🖀 *buses 4, 7, 10, 13, 14, 31, 32 and 33; open: Mon–Sat; reservations recommended; all credit cards accepted; Tuscan;* ❷❸. If you're finding the conference food a bit bland and predictable, you should consider this friendly but unpretentious trattoria, conveniently located near the Palazzo degli Affari. A real shot in the arm, it will not only rekindle your tastebuds

CAFFÈ CONCERTO
Ristorante

LUNGARNO C. COLOMB

but will acquaint you with the flavoursome glories of traditional Tuscan cooking: *zuppa di faro, panzanella, tagliatelle con salsa dei funghi, trippa alla fiorentina*, you'll find them all here. No surprises admittedly but no unwelcome offerings either.

• **Hemingway** *Pza Piattellina 9r; ✆ 055 284781;* 🚌 *bus D; open: Tue–Sun 1800–0200; reservations unnecessary; all credit cards accepted; International;* ❶❷. This bar-brasserie is located in the Oltrarno, near the church of Santa Maria del Carmine – famous for the Brancacci chapel with breathtaking frescos by Masaccio and Masolino. Friendly and relaxed, it's the perfect place to unwind after a long day. While sipping a cocktail you can choose from the appetising light dishes on offer – quiches, salamis, fish dishes (including oysters), fresh salads and a range of Italian and foreign cheeses. On Tuesdays, Thursdays and Fridays the theme is ethnic food from around the world.

• **Hotel Excelsior** *Pza Ognissanti; ✆ 055 264201;* 🚌 *buses 12 and B; open: daily 1200–1430, 1900–2300; reservations recommended; all credit cards accepted; Italian;* ❶❷❸. The Excelsior is Florence's most exclusive hotel and the lavish surroundings of the Sala Vespucci can hardly fail to impress. (You can hire a private room if you wish.) The hotel kitchens cater with business men and women in mind, and there are specially designed 'working lunch' menus. The style of cooking owes a good deal to French traditions though not without Tuscan influences. A typical dinner might consist of shrimps and white bean salad, wholemeal pasta in wild mushroom sauce, capon bread stuffed with mashed spring onions, followed by mousse of green lemon. On Sundays there's a lively buffet brunch complete with jazz band.

The hotel kitchens cater with business men and women in mind, and there are specially designed 'working lunch' menus.

• **Lo Strettoio** *V. di Serpiolle 7; ✆ 055 4250044;* 🚌 *buses 14 and 43; open: Tue–Sat 1200– 1430, 1900–2300; reservations recommended; all credit cards accepted; Tuscan-Italian;* ❶❷❸. Located in the Serpiolle district on the northern edge of town, you'll appreciate why Lo Strettoio is worth the drive when you arrive. The restaurant incorporates the remains of a 17th-century winepress and there are wonderful views of Florence from the terrace. The cooking more than lives up to raised expectations. You can opt either for the all-inclusive *menù degustazione* or choose from the à la carte. Lentil, potato and barley soup, spaghetti with rabbit and courgette flowers and lasagne with asparagus and pecorino cheese make way for spiced guinea fowl and pigeon stuffed with plums in a brandy sauce. If you're so inclined, round off your meal with a shot of grappa – there are 300 varieties to choose from.

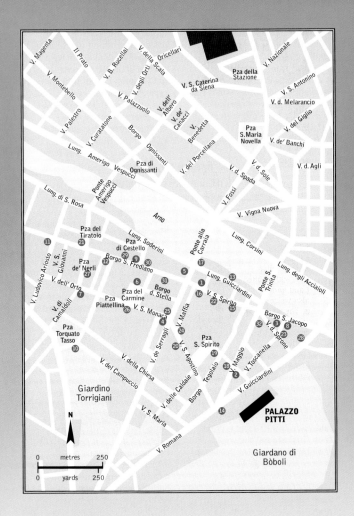

Santo Spirito

The Oltrarno (*see also pages 8–15*) incorporates the old working-class districts of San Frediano and Santo Spirito, where there's a tiny market most days. Many of the eateries here are family-run and patronised by local people.

SANTO SPIRITO
Restaurants

Angiolino ❶

V. Santo Spirito 36r

✆ 055 2398976

🚍 Buses 6 and D

Open: daily 1200–1430, 1900–2230

Reservations recommended

All credit cards accepted

Tuscan

❶❷

Popular with locals (especially on Sunday for the family lunch), this spacious cellar restaurant with vaulted ceiling and antique stove also welcomes tourists. The waiters are happy to recommend the house specialities, which include the starter *pappa al pomodoro* and *rognoncini di vitello* (veal kidneys).

La Baruciola ❷

V. Maggio 61r

✆ 055 218906

🚍 Buses 11, 36 and 37

Open: daily 1200–1430, 1900–2230

Reservations recommended

All credit cards accepted

Tuscan-Italian

❶❷

Popular with tourists, especially Americans, this friendly trattoria makes an ideal lunch stop if you've just been browsing in the local antique shops; it's livelier in the evenings,

however. The manager, whose twin brother is the chef, will guide you through the menu of fish and meat dishes. You might start with *crostone di cavolo nero* (toasted bread with black cabbage), followed by *fegato* (liver), or opt for the trout fillet or grilled salmon, while for vegetarians there's a tasty lasagne.

Camillo ❸

Borgo S. Jacopo 57r

✆ 055 212427

🚍 Bus D

Open: daily 1200–1430, 1900–2300

Reservations recommended

All credit cards accepted

Tuscan-Italian

❶❷

A large trattoria, often busy, where guests sit elbow to elbow. Extensive menu with main courses including Florentine standards such as *bistecca* and *trippa alla fiorentina*, but also fish dishes – salmon and sole predominantly.

Cavolo Nero ❹

V. del' Ardiglione 22

✆ 055 294744

🚍 Buses 11, 36, 37 and D

▲ Angiolino

well as *calzone* (pasty) and other dishes including *ravioli alla crema di tartufo* (ravioli in cream of mushroom sauce), scampi, shrimps and asparagus with curry and grills including beef fillet.

Dolce Vita ❻

Pza del Carmine 5	
ℭ 055 280018	
🚍 Buses 6 and D	
Open: daily 1900–2330	
Reservations unnecessary	
All credit cards accepted	
Tuscan	
❷❷	

A trendy venue, popular with bright young things who like to dress up, this restaurant-bar offers a small but pleasingly inventive choice of Florentine dishes.

Il Guscio ❼

V. dell' Orto 49	
ℭ 055 224421	
🚍 Bus D	
Open: Tue–Sat 1930–2300	
Reservations essential	
All credit cards accepted	
Italian	
❷❷	

'The Shell' offers tasty *casalinga* dishes from all over Italy. High points include home-made ravioli, mushroom soup and spaghetti with anchovies for starters with equally tasty *secondi* to follow, including *lampredotto* (a kind of tripe) served with artichokes, or more conventional meat courses if you prefer.

Open: daily 1900–2400	
Reservations recommended	
No credit cards accepted	
Tuscan	
❸❸❸	

This increasingly fashionable eatery has a nice location just off Piazza del Carmine. The team of chefs pride themselves on their inventive approach to Tuscan cuisine – the 'must tries' include the smoked salmon and the ravioli with a pesto made from black cabbage (*cavolo nero*). All the pastas are homemade and the second courses include fresh fish as well as meat dishes. Try to save room for a dessert. For romantics, dinner is by candlelight.

Dante ❺

Pza Nazzario Sauro 12	
ℭ 055 293215	
🚍 Buses 6 and D	
Open: daily 1200–1430, 1900–2230	
Reservations unnecessary	
All credit cards accepted	
Tuscan-Italian	
❷❷	

Friendly trattoria near the Ponte alla Carraia, offering a selection of 25 pizza toppings as

An added attraction is the choice of wines – there are more than 50 varieties to choose from.

Osteria del Cinghiale Bianco ❽

Borgo S. Jacopo 43r	
✆ 055 215706	
🚍 Bus D	
Open: Thu–Mon 1200–1430, 1900–2230	
Reservations unnecessary	
No credit cards accepted	
Tuscan	
€€	

Only a stone's throw from the Ponte Vecchio and opposite the church of San Jacopo Sopr' Arno, this popular *osteria* is located in a medieval tower. The staff are friendly and laid-back, the food, wholesome and tasty. You can opt for a dish of the day or a fixed price menu comprising two courses and a quarter litre of wine.

Sabatino ❾

Borgo S. Frediano 39r	
✆ 055 284625	
🚍 Buses 6 and D	
Open: Mon–Fri	
Reservations essential	
No credit cards accepted	
Tuscan	
€–€€	

This homely, family-run trattoria in the Oltrarno is small and very popular. Sabatino has been around for more than half a century and still relies on its reputation for good, no-frills home cooking. The tiled interior has a certain period charm.

Al Tranvai ❿

Pza Torquato Tasso 14r	
✆ 055 225197	
🚍 Buses 12 and 13	
Open: Mon–Fri 1200–1500, 1900–2230	
Reservations unnecessary	
No credit cards accepted	
Tuscan	
€–€€	

A cheap and cheerful eatery near the old tram terminus, hence the name. Play safe with the meatballs in tomato sauce, or be more adventurous and opt for tripe salad or giblets. You eat shoulder to shoulder with fellow diners, mainly hard-up students. A few outside tables.

Alla Vecchia Bettola ⓫

Vle Ludovico Ariosto 43/5	
✆ 055 288383	
🚍 Buses 6 and D	
Open: Tue–Sat 0730–1530, 1930–2230	
Reservations unnecessary	
All credit cards accepted	
Tuscan	
€€	

The menu changes every day at this convivial eatery near the Porta San Frediano, but you can usually count on something traditional, for example bean soup, dumplings with rabbit sauce, or carpaccio (beef slices). Save room for the *cantuccini* (almond biscuits) washed down ideally with a glass of Vin Santo. A carafe of red or white wine is brought automatically to your table and you'll be charged according to how much you drink. Some outside seating.

OSTERIA DEL CINGHIALE BIANCO

SANTO SPIRITO
Bars, cafés and pubs

L'Antico Borgo 12

Borgo S. Frediano 55

⊘ None available

🚍 Buses 6 and D

Open: Mon–Sat 0630–2100

€

Small bar with tables at the rear, where you can buy pastries, sandwiches, croissants and other snacks as well as coffee, beer, wines and spirits.

Beccofino 13

Pza degli Scarlatti

☎ 055 290076

🚍 Buses 6 and D

Open: wine bar 1130–1500, 1600–2400; restaurant 1200–1430, 1900–2300

€€

This American-style wine bar, on the embankment (Lungarno Guicciardini) between Ponte alla Carraia and Ponte S. Trinita, offers stylish versions of traditional Tuscan dishes. Wine is served by the glass as well as by the bottle, so this is a good place to sample rival Chiantis.

Bianchi 14

Pza S. Felice 3

⊘ None available

🚍 Buses 11, 36, 37 and D

Open: Mon–Sat 0700–0100

€

Small, traditional café opposite the church of San Felice, with a counter selling sandwiches, pastries, *crostini* (toasted bread), pâtés and other snacks. Drinks include beers and cocktails.

Bistro 15

V. Santo Spirito 60

☎ 055 211264

🚍 Buses 6 and D

Open: daily 1200–1430, 1930–2300

€–€€

Wooden table, benches and photographs of old Florence add to the appeal of this old-fashioned *fiaschetteria*. The simple menu, consisting of *antipasti* and *primi* – bread with oil, *pasta corta con pomodoro*, *pesto alla Genovese*, roast beef, cheese, and so on – is chalked on a board or scribbled on paper napkins.

Borgo Antico 16

Pza Santo Spirito 6r

☎ 055 210437

🚍 Bus D

Open: daily 1245–1430, 1945–2400

€€

Noisy, popular trattoria with a reputation for gruff service and hearty helpings of pasta and other traditional Italian dishes. Among the more unusual items on the menu are baked guinea hen with roast potatoes and baked sea bass. If you're a pizza fan, you'll appreciate the variety of toppings and the gratifyingly crisp bases. Outside tables in the piazza.

Café Soderini 17

Pza Nazzario Sauro 18

⊘ None available

🚍 Buses 6 and D

Open: Mon–Sat 0800–2000

€

Café on the corner of Lungarno Guicciardini where the filled rolls are named after the stars. The Julia Roberts, for example, consists of *bresaola* (salted beef slices) and cheese with salad, while the Tina Turner is a feisty mix of tuna, tomato and mayonaise.

La Casalinga 18

V. dei Michelozzi 9r

☎ 055 218624

🚍 Buses 11, 36 and 37

Open: daily 1200–1430, 1900–2300

€€

A popular lunch spot with local workers, this modern trattoria deals in typical Tuscan dishes such as *ribollita*, *bollito di manzo* (boiled beef) and *coniglio al forno* (roast rabbit); also soups.

PopCafé 🄆

Pza Santo Spirito 18a/r

✆ 055 111201

🚍 Bus D

Open: daily 0900–2400

€

A new kid on the block, this modern bar doubles as an internet café – you can send an e-mail while sipping a fruit juice or a beer in a deliberately low-key atmosphere, intended to remind you of your kitchen or living room. Occasional small exhibitions and themed tasting evenings. Note that this is a club, so you have to pay the annual membership effectively as a cover charge.

San Agostino 🄦

V. S. Agostino 23

✆ None available

🚍 Bus D

Open: daily 1130–1400, 1900–2230

€

Cheap and cheerful trattoria, rustling up a small range of pizzas. Alternatively, there's a menu of the day and a three-course, fixed price lunch.

San Onofrio 🄧

V. S. Onofrio 20–2

✆ None available

🚍 Bus D

Open: daily 0900–1430, 1600–2000

€

Coffee shop with tearoom by the Porta San Frediano, selling cakes and a selection of sandwiches; also ice cream.

Santo Spirito 🄨

V. Santo Spirito 10

✆ None available

🚍 Buses 6 and D

Open: daily 0700–2030

€

Small café, where locals drop in to read the newspapers over a coffee and snack.

Le Torri 🄩

V. de' Ramaglianti 2

✆ None available

🚍 Buses 11, 36 and 37

Open: daily 0800–2230

€

Neighbourhood café with a snack bar, selling pizza slices, salads (chicken, mozzarella and tomato), roast beef, cured ham, and so on.

SANTO SPIRITO
Shops, markets and picnic sites

Bakeries, confectioners and pasta shops

Agostino Pasticceria 24

V. S. Agostino 38

🚍 Bus D

Open: Tue–Sun 0600–2400

Cake shop specialising in *schiacciata alla fiorentina* (iced sponge cake), *fritelle* (sugary batter biscuits) and *bomboloni* (doughnuts), piping hot if you happen to arrive around 1600.

La Bolognese 25

V. de Serragli 24

🚍 Buses 11, 36 and 37

Open: Mon–Sat 0700–1300, 1630–1930, closed Wed pm

Fresh pasta for sale, with interesting varieties such as ravioli with truffles or pumpkin, and *torellini* with smoked salmon. *Gnocchi* (dumplings) are also available.

Quattrocchi 26

V. Santa Monaca 3r

🚍 Buses 6 and D

Open: daily 0700–1930

This bakery sells a range of breads from the unsalted Tuscan variety to *schiacciata* (flat bread with oil); also pizzas.

Delicatessens and grocers

Coloniali 27

Pza dei Nerli 10

🚍 Buses 6 and D

Open: Mon–Sat 0815–1245, 1530–1930

A small grocery store on the corner of the square, selling sweets

▲ Santo Spirito Market

and biscuits as well as ground coffees.

Delicatesse Azzarri Paolo

Borgo S. Jacopo 27b–c

🚌 Bus D

Open: daily 0800–2000

Though it describes itself as a delicatessen, this is really a general store. Packed to the rafters with groceries, fruit, vegetables (including packs of salad) and wines, there are also well-stocked meat and deli counters.

La Dispensa 28

V. Barbadori 26r

🚌 Bus D

Open: daily 0800–2000

You can buy fresh milk here as well as a variety of typical Tuscan produce – everything from wines and olives to salami, yoghurt, pecorino cheese and *crostini*.

Latteria 29

Borgo S. Frediano 52

🚌 Buses 6 and D

Open: daily 0800–1300, 1600–1930

While it's nothing special, this little shop is handy for fresh milk and groceries if you happen to be in the vicinity.

Migrana 30

Borgo S. Frediano 81/83r

🚌 Buses 6 and D

Open: daily 0800–1330, 1630–2000

Full of gastronomic delights, Migrana must rate as the best delicatessen this side of the river. Among the speciality cheeses, look out for gorgonzola *al mascarpone*, and cheese with truffles and ricotta. Then there are the yoghurts, fruit, extra virgin olive oils, wines (including Brunello and Vin Santo) and imported beers (Becks).

Paolo e Marla 25

V. de Serragli 24

🚌 Buses 11, 36 and 37

Open: daily 0730–1400, 1600–2000, closed Wed pm

An Aladdin's cave, the shelves tightly packed with groceries, wines, oils, dried beans and rice. Hams hang overhead and a delicatessen counter is stocked with cheeses, olives, salami and other delicacies.

Prodotti Tipici Toscani 3

Borgo S. Jacopo 3

🚌 Bus D

Open: daily 0730–1400, 1630–2000

This local store has been selling typical Italian produce since it was established in 1928. Apart from Chianti Classico and other Tuscan wines, there's an excellent selection of cheeses, salamis and extra virgin olive oils, including Rocca di Montegrossi. There's even an ice-cream counter!

La Torinese 31

Borgo S. Frediano 128

🚌 Buses 6 and D

Open: daily 0800–1300, 1630–2000

Patisserie specialising in Tuscan *panforte* (a delicious cake filled with almonds and dried fruit), *torroncini* (sweets), biscuits, wines and, more unusually, American muffins.

Wine and oils

Paolo Peri 32

V. Maggio 5r

🚌 Buses 11, 36 and 37

Open: daily 0800–1300, 1600–2000

This excellent wine shop with a stock in excess of 20,000 bottles is the perfect port of call for Chianti lovers. You can, for example, pick up an Antinori label quite cheaply and the Verazzano, Fontodi and Frescobaldi are all competitively priced. If your budget can run to a Brunello di Montalcino, reckoned to be among the best Italian wines, so much the better. Also on sale is a grappa di Brunello, as well as a range of home-grown sparkling wines: Asti, Ferrari Brut and Marchese Antinori. The shop is equally hot on virgin olive oils – the Fantoio di Santa Tea can be recommended.

Tuscan cuisine

Robust, no-nonsense cooking

If you've ever eaten at a French restaurant you'll probably be familiar with *canard à l'orange*, *soupe à l'oignon*, *sauce béchamel* and crêpes. What you may not know is that the recipes for all these dishes originated in Tuscany and were introduced to the French court by **Caterina de' Medici**, wife of Henri of Navarre, in the 16th century. Catherine's favourite dish was *cibrèo*, a stew made from the less appetising parts of a chicken (gizzard, liver, neck, even the comb, which were fried with onions then mixed with egg yolk, lemon and ginger). It's rarely found nowadays even in Tuscany, but the name is preserved in one of Florence's most adventurous gourmet restaurants as it's this dish that epitomises the best Tuscan cooking, the tradition known as *casalinga*.

Today's chefs are trying to recreate or adapt old family recipes for dishes which fell into abeyance in the over-refined 18th century, but which never fell from grace in the kitchens of the Tuscan countryside. **Casalinga** is robust, no-nonsense cooking – the emphasis is on improvisation using the ingredients that are to hand, waste of any kind being frowned on and hurrying forbidden. These culinary virtues are exemplified in two popular soups, *ribollita* and *pappa al pomodoro*, both made with stale bread (*pappa*). (Note that Tuscan bread is unsalted – the poet Dante complained in exile about the salty taste of 'foreign' bread.) *Pappa* is allowed to soften until it is a mushy pulp before it is heated in a saucepan with ripe tomatoes, garlic, pepper and basil, while the bread in *ribollita* is soaked in a stew containing the kind of nourishing vegetables that sustained agricultural workers through the hard winter: onions, celery, carrots, peas, potatoes, and black cabbage (*cavolo nero*). White *cannellini* beans are another important ingredient in soups – not for nothing were the Florentines nicknamed 'bean eaters'! Meat dishes too leave nothing to waste. Kidneys are stewed with garlic and tomatoes, liver is cooked with sage, while tripe is used not only in the celebrated *trippa alla fiorentina* but as a filling in sandwiches.

In Tuscan cuisine **the countryside** is seen as an infinite resource. Florentines head for the woods in search of *porcini* mushrooms and the much-loved truffles (*tartufo*) – the best are found in Montaione between Florence and Pisa where a festival is held at the end of October. Both the red and black varieties of Tuscan pig are used to make salami (ideally flavoured with fennel seeds), while sausages and salty *casentino* ham often appear among the *antipasti* on restaurant menus. **Wild boar** were reintroduced in the 1960s and have reproduced so successfully that the traditional dish *cinghiale alla Maremmana*, is again appearing on the menus of the more enterprising restaurants.

Rabbit, stuffed and cooked in the oven, is another favourite; hare is less common, with the notable exception of the piquant first course, *pappardelle alla lepre*. Surprisingly, *bistecca alla fiorentina*, now regarded as the quintessential Tuscan dish is English in origin – *bistecca* derives from beefsteak and was recreated to please British tourists in the 18th century. Any *bistecca* worth its salt must be made from Chianina cows, raised in the Chiano valley near Arrezzo. Two or three inches thick, it should be grilled over an open flame and served blood rare.

While Tuscan cuisine is mainly meat-based, this doesn't mean that fish doesn't get a look in. The most common dish is *baccalà*, (salted dried cod, usually casseroled with onions in a tomato sauce). A more succulent dish is *calamari in inzimino*, a spicy stew made from squid, spinach and chard.

If you don't have a sweet tooth you'll most likely want to round off your meal with cheese. In Tuscany this must be pecorino, made from sheeps' milk – the sheep are fed on the lush grass of the *crete senese*, the 'land of clay'.

> **The emphasis is on improvisation using the ingredients that are to hand, waste of any kind being frowned on and hurrying forbidden.**

• **Cibrèo** *V. dei Macci 118r; ✆ 055 2341110; ⓫ bus 14; open: Tue–Sat 1200–1430, 1930–2300; reservations essential; all credit cards accepted; Tuscan;* €€–€€€. One of the city's most popular eateries and arguably the best venue in Florence for trying Tuscan cuisine, Cibrèo is owned by Fabio Picchi who's been in the business more than 20 years. The ambience is relaxed and convivial, the décor restrained, yet refined. There's no written menu; instead a waitress will explain the dishes to you. These may include yellow pepper soup, corn mush with black cabbage, stuffed neck of hen, pigeon stuffed with Crimona mustard, or veal and ricotta croquettes. Book as many days in advance as possible.

▲ *Bistecca alla fiorentina*

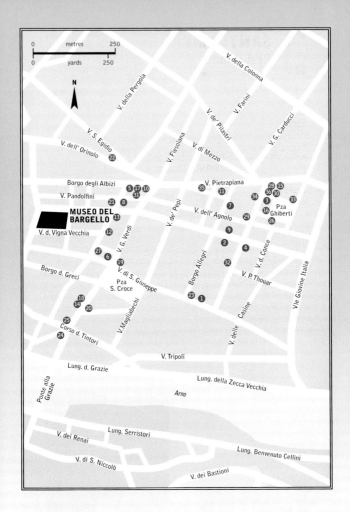

Sant' Ambrogio

At the heart of this area is Florence's second market, named after the ancient church of Sant' Ambrogio. The eateries cluster around the market and along Via Ghibellina, a street of handsome palaces, including the former home of Michelangelo (Casa Buonarroti).

SANT' AMBROGIO
Restaurants

Baldovino ❶

V. di S. Giuseppe 22r

✆ 055 241773

🚌 Bus C

Open: Tue–Sun 1200–1430, 1900–2400

Reservations recommended

All credit cards accepted

Tuscan-Italian

❷❷

Owned by Scotsman David Gardner, this pizzeria-restaurant almost on the doorstep of Santa Croce is winning accolades for its fresh-faced approach to traditional Tuscan cuisine. Fish is another strong point, while the pizzas (cooked in a wood-fired oven) are available at lunch as well as in the evenings.

La Baraonda ❷

V. Ghibellina 67r

✆ 055 2341171

🚌 Bus 14

Open: Mon–Sat 1200–1430, 1900–2300, closed Mon lunch

Reservations recommended

All credit cards accepted

Tuscan

❷❸

The authentic Florentine dishes include a tasty *farinata di cavolo nero* (wheaten black cabbage soup), as well as *coniglio* (rabbit), *anatra arosto* (roast duck) and the *pièce de résistance*, *coscio di maiale al latte con salsa di mela* (leg of pork in milk with apple sauce). Good choice of Tuscan wines.

Cibrèo ❸

V. Andrea del Verrocchio 5r

✆ 055 2345853

🚌 Bus 14

Open: Tue–Sat 1230–1430, 1930–2300

No reservations allowed

All credit cards accepted

Tuscan

❷❷

Sibling of the Cibrèo restaurant just across the street (*see page 27*), Cibrèo mark 2 serves from the same menu in more humble surroundings and at reduced prices – for this reason it's known as the 'poor people's room' (*sala dei poveri*). No bookings are taken and you'll almost certainly have to queue.

▲ Baldovino

Dino

V. Ghibellina 51r
✆ 055 241452
🚍 Bus 14
Open: Tue–Sun 1230–1430, 1930–2230, closed Sun evening
Reservations recommended
All credit cards accepted
Tuscan
€€

Spacious and well lit, Dino's offers a formal dining experience without having to pay over the odds. All the dishes are prepared with due care and attention, producing excellent results. Try the *straccotta del granduca* (beef cooked slowly in red Chianti wine with raisins and pinenuts), *fileto di manzo in salsa alle nocci* (beef fillet cooked rare in a cream red wine and walnut sauce) or the stewed rabbit with tomato and black and green olives. Group bookings are encouraged in July and August, so if you're looking for intimacy, this may not be the place for you.

I Ghibellini

Pza S. Pier Maggiore 8–10
✆ 055 214424
🚍 Bus A
Open: Thu–Tue 1200–1600, 1700–0030
Reservations unnecessary
All credit cards accepted
Tuscan
€€

The pleasing interior design makes good use of the medieval brick-work – the building dates from the 14th century and the downstairs room was once the wine cellar. The cuisine too is traditional Tuscan, although many visitors are more attracted by the pizzas (50 different toppings and small and large sizes) and by the lunchtime buffet. Large modern terrace for summer dining.

Leo

V. Torta 7r
✆ 055 210829
🚍 Bus 23
Open: Tue–Sun 1200–1500, 1900–2400
Reservations unnecessary
All credit cards accepted
Tuscan
€€

A modern, fairly formal *ristorante* offering a rather predictable range of Tuscan dishes, but none the worse for that. Start with the carpaccio (slices of raw beef), then follow with the *ossobuco alla fiorentina* (veal stew in tomato sauce). There are also several grill options.

Masticabrodo ⑦

Borgo Allegri 58r
✆ 055 241920
🚍 Bus C
Open: Mon–Sat 1200–1430, 1900–2300
Reservations recommended
All credit cards accepted
Tuscan
€

Small unpretentious eatery near Piazza dei Ciompi, specialising in basic Tuscan appetisers and first courses, for example *bruschette* (toasted bread with oil), *salumi* (salami), *pappa al pomodoro* (spicy bread and tomato soup) and *gnocchi al gorgonzola* (dumplings in gorgonzola cheese sauce).

Mastro Ciliegia ⑧

V. Matteo Palmieri 34r
✆ 055 293372
🚍 Buses 14 and A
Open: Tue–Sun 1200–1430, 2000–2400
Reservations unnecessary
💳 American Express
Tuscan-Italian
€€

▲ Piazza Santa Croce

Lively trattoria, very popular with young people, especially in the evenings, and good value. Menu includes pizzas, grilled meats and Tuscan standards. The real bargain is the pizza and beer combination.

Alle Murate 🟨

V. Ghibellina 52–4r

✆ 055 240618

🚍 Bus 14

Open: daily 1830–2300

Reservations recommended

All credit cards accepted

Tuscan

🟡🟡–🟡🟡🟡

At this decidedly up-market *vineria* (the choice of wines currently runs to around 140) with a restaurant next door, Umberto Montano's stylish establishment offers some of the best regional cuisine in the city. The highlights include *brasato di Chianina al Brunello di Montalcino* (best Chianina beef, braised in wine) and *stufato di agnello alla pastorale* (lamb stew). Also worth noting are the desserts – try the *pan di zucchero e cioccolata calda* (sugared bread and hot chocolate). The ambience is perfect for a romantic dinner *à deux*.

Natalino 🟨

Borgo degli Albizi 17r

✆ 055 289404

🚍 Bus A

Open: Tue–Sun 1200–1430, 1900–2300

Reservations recommended

All credit cards accepted

Tuscan

🟡🟡

Humble but engaging *osteria*, friendly and busy, offering a basic Tuscan menu, for example grilled chicken, rabbit 'house style', escalope and the usual range of *primi* and *antipasti*.

TRATTORIA

Tirabusciò
DI ROBERTO MAURRI

Orient Express ⓫

Borgo Allegri 9r	
✆ 055 2469028	
🚌 Bus C	
Open: daily 1200–1430, 1900–2300	
Reservations recommended	
All credit cards accepted	
International	
⓰⓰–⓰⓰⓰	

Somewhere to take a partner if you want to impress them with your culinary knowledge and sophistication. Look particularly to the Russian and Georgian specialities, where the emphasis is on *zakuski* (starters), in this case mainly seafood – prawns laced with vodka, pickled herring, and so on. Order from the wine menu or try a flavoured vodka.

Osteria del Caffè Italiano ⓬

V. Isola delle Stinche 11–13	
✆ 055 289368	
🚌 Buses 14, 23 and A	
Open: Tue–Sun 1000–2400	
Reservations recommended	
All credit cards accepted	
Tuscan	
⓰⓰	

Favoured by patrons of the nearby Teatro Verdi,

this restaurant doubles as a wine bar so you can either make do with a snack, or go for the full Tuscan blow-out! You could start, for example, with a bean soup and follow with pork chop Sienese-style. Good selection of Tuscan wines, by the bottle or glass.

Pallotino ⓭

V. Isola delle Stinche 1r	
✆ 055 289573	
🚌 Bus 23	
Open: Tue–Sun 1230–1430, 1930–2215	
Reservations unnecessary	
No credit cards accepted	
Italian	
⓰	

Mainstream trattoria, not far from the Bargello. Lacks atmosphere in the evenings, but could be useful for lunch. The menu is straightforward: mainly pasta dishes to start – though there's also a tasty leek and bean soup – with the likes of roast turkey, tomato and spinach to follow.

Il Tirabusciò ⓮

V. dei Benci 34r	
✆ 055 2476225	

🚌 Buses 23 and B	
Open: Fri–Tue 1200–1430, 1830–2200	
Reservations unnecessary	
💳 💳	
Tuscan	
⓰⓰	

A useful option at midday if you're looking for an invigorating light lunch: *antipasto* or salad, followed by a choice of first courses, fruit or dessert. In the evenings there's a tourist menu, or you can select from the à la carte dishes which include a good *zuppa di faro* (wheat soup), while the *baccalà alla livornese* (salted cod Livorno-style) is delicious. Pleasant and cosy with candlelit tables. Another plus is the vegetarian menu, for example, risotto with herbs or spaghetti in oil.

Vecchio Mercato ⓯

Borgo la Croce 45	
✆ 055 2456660	
🚌 Buses A and C	
Open: daily 0730–2200	
Reservations unnecessary	
No credit cards accepted	
Tuscan-Italian	
⓰	

Local workers and businessmen drop in here for breakfast on the way to work. At lunchtimes hot food is served from 1230 until 1430. There's a set menu and a menu of the day, revolving around pasta dishes and other Italian standards. Also ice creams.

SANT' AMBROGIO
Bars, cafés and pubs

L'Agnolo della Pizza ⑯

V. dell' Agnolo, corner of V. Mino

✆ None available

🚌 Bus C

Open: Mon–Sat 0800–1430, 1530–1930

€

Small pizzeria, catering mainly for takeaway customers with the offer of a free drink with every slice. The speciality of the house is *focaccia con nutela*.

Antico Noè ⑰

Volta S. Pier Maggiore 6r

✆ 055 2340838

🚌 Bus A

Open: Mon–Sat 1200–1430, 1800–2230

€

This is a tiny *mescita* or wine shop with tiled walls and room only for a handful of tables. Most people come here for a glass of Chianti and a sandwich (bread rolls to order) or snack: choose from salami, tripe, cheese, *crostini*, cold cuts, sausage and marinated vegetables.

Balducci ⑱

V. dei Benci 7

✆ None available

🚌 Bus 23

Open: daily 1200–1430, 1800–2100

€

Traditional wine bar with small wooden tables, rush chairs and a marble counter. Customers leaf through the newspaper while sipping a glass of Chianti and there's a deli counter serving snacks.

Boccadama ⑲

Pza S. Croce 26r

✆ 055 243640

🚌 Bus 23

Open: Tue–Sun 0830–2400

€€

Stylish wine bar where you can enjoy a refreshing light meal (lunch or dinner). There's an excellent range of salamis and Italian and French cheeses, also wonderful salads. Some outside seating overlooking the church of Santa Croce.

Le Colonnine ⑳

V. dei Benci 6r

✆ 055 2346417

🚌 Bus 23

Open: Tue–Sun 0800–2200

€

Situated in a beautiful medieval building – the classical pillars supporting the canopy give it its name – this large café has a snack area to the front and restaurant seating for the pizzeria at the rear.

Danny Rock ㉑

V. Pandolfini 13r

✆ 055 2340307

🚌 Buses 14 and A

Open: daily 1200–1500, 1900–0100 (Sat until 0200)

€

This brash, American-style bar seems to appeal mainly to foreigners and is nearly always full to overflowing, especially at weekends. The mixture of food is unusual and includes pizzas, crêpes and *galettes* (pancakes), burgers, and

salads with various sauces. Cocktails are the other speciality.

Eby's 22

V. S. Egidio 1

☎ None available

🚌 Buses 14 and 23

Open: Thu–Tue 0800–0100

€

A small café-bar, specialising in kosher snacks. A local rabbi guarantees all sandwich fillings and pancakes; cheeses and ice creams (generous helpings) are also on sale.

Enoteca Baldovino 23

V. di S. Giuseppe 18r

☎ 055 2347220

🚌 Bus C

Open: Tue–Sun 1200–2400

€ €

A relative of the restaurant of the same name, this wine bar also serves snacks and appetisers including *crostini*, filled rolls, cheeses and salami.

Kikuya 24

V. dei Benci 43r

☎ 055 2344879

🚌 Bus 23

Open: Wed–Mon 1900–0230

€

Tiny, late-night cocktail bar also selling draught beers (Red Stripe, Fargo and Bombadier Charles Wells). The noise can be unbearable when the live bands perform; otherwise the entertainment takes the form of live sport on widescreen TV. Happy hour runs from 1900 to 2200 (snacks at half price).

Red Garter 25

V. dei Benci 33r

☎ 055 2344904

🚌 Bus 23

Open: Tue–Sun 1000–0100

€

Long-established (1962) and popular American bar with live music and a good line in cocktails. Draught beers include McFarland, Heineken and Coors. Happy hour 2000–2130 (until 2100 Fri and Sat).

Union 26

V. Mino 8r

☎ None available

🚌 Bus 14

Open: daily 0700–2000

€

Humble stand-up café and bar frequented by traders from Sant' Ambrogio Market. Sells snacks including pastries.

Vivoli 27

V. Isola delle Stinche 7r

☎ 055 292334

🚌 Bus 14

Open: daily 0800–2000

€

This unpretentious ice-cream parlour is one of the best in Florence. The flavours include amaretto, chocolate mousse, trifle, orange cream, even rice pudding! Point to what you want at the counter and the assistant will mix-and-match for you. Prices vary depending on the number of scoops you choose.

SANT' AMBROGIO
Shops, markets and picnic sites

Bakeries, confectioners and pasta shops

La Pagnotta 28

Borgo la Croce 109

🚍 Buses A and C

Open: daily 0700–1300, 1600–1930

Bakery on the corner of Via dei Macci, selling fresh Tuscan loaves, *grissini* (bread sticks), pastries and biscuits.

Pane e focacce 29

V. dei Macci 65r

🚍 Bus B

Open: daily 0700–1300, 1600–1930

Baker's shop close to the Sant' Ambrogio Market. Buy some delicious, coarse Florentine bread to eat with salami.

Delicatessens and grocers

Alimentari 30

V. Andrea del Verrocchio 8r

🚍 Bus 14

Open: daily 0800–1300, 1630–2000

Grocery outlet selling Tuscan produce. It's owned by Fabio Picchi of the Cibrèo restaurant.

Grana Market 31

Pza S. Pier Maggiore 4r

🚍 Bus A

Open: daily 0600–1615, 1930–2100, closed Wed pm

A delightful grocery store, run on traditional lines (cured hams hanging from racks on the ceiling, for example). It sells wines, olive oils and cereals and there's an excellent deli counter.

Latteria 32

V. dei Macci 33

🚍 Bus 14

Open: daily 0800–1300, 1600–2000

Neighbourhood dairy selling milk, cheese and groceries; also a small selection of wines.

Salumeria 34

V. dei Macci 117

🚍 Bus 14

Open: daily 0800–1300, 1630–2000

Useful delicatessen near the Sant' Ambrogio Market. The locals make a beeline for the fish fillets, displayed in marble tanks, while there's also a good choice of ham, cheeses, salami, fresh pasta, olives and oils.

Standa 35

V. Pietrapiana 46

🚍 Bus B

Open: daily 0800–2000

Branch of the Italian supermarket chain, handy for buying Italian wines, oils, olives and preserves.

Tripe stall 36

On Via dei Macci, in front of **La Pagnotta** bakery and next door to **Cibrèo** restaurant (*see page 27*).

Markets

Mercato di Sant' Ambrogio 33

Pza Ghiberti

🚍 Bus B

Open: Mon–Sat 0700–1400

This busy produce market is located in an ageing 19th-century hall. Cheese, salami, ham, meat and fish can be found inside while the square fills with stalls selling fruit and vegetables, some of it organic.

▲ Mercato di Sant' Ambrogio

Chianti

Drinking through dynasties

Take the local train from Florence to Siena and you will see some of the loveliest countryside in Europe – a green landscape of gently undulating hills, planted with vineyards and olive groves as far as the eye can see, and above them the crenellated walls of castles founded in the Middle Ages. 'Chianti country' has been synonymous with wine growing since at least the 14th century; one of its earliest champions was the wealthy merchant, **Francesco di Marco Datini**, more famous as the inventor of the Bill of Exchange.

Today there are around 7000 producers in what is now Italy's largest wine growing region. For purposes of classification, it's divided into eight areas, the most important of which is **Chianti Classico** – all bottles produced here carry the emblem of the black cockerel (*gallo nero*), originally the symbol of a medieval defensive league formed against Siena. The top three dozen or so producers, many of whom were responsible for rescuing Chianti from the doldrums in the 1960s and 1970s, belong to a consortium which aims to promote the best wines. The leading estates include Fontodi, Verazzano, Monsanto, Isola e Olena, Castello di Brolio and Passignano, the property of the **Antinori family**. The founder

of this dynasty, Giovanni di Piero Antinori, first enters the records of the Florentine Vintners' Guild in 1385. The family sold their wines from a shop in the grounds of their splendid Renaissance *palazzo* in Via Tornabuoni. In 1966 descendants of Antinori opened a restaurant here which is open to the public (*see page 37*). You can buy wines from all their estates, including their most recent acquisition, Atlas Peaks in Napa Valley, California.

Chianti wine is derived from the Sangiovese grape, which thrives on a shaley clay known as *galestro*. It was in the 1850s that Count Bettino Ricasoli of Castello di Brolio hit on the successful formula of blending **Sangiovese** with three other grapes – **Malvasia**, **Trebbiano** and **Canaiolo Nero**. Recently, experiments have been made with imported varieties including Cabernet Sauvignon, Chardonnay and Syrah. A good Chianti is bright ruby in colour and full-bodied with a strong bouquet. One of its beauties is its flexibility: it can accompany and complement anything from pasta dishes to poultry, grilled and roast meats, game, and even cheese.

Below are some of the many places where you can buy Chianti wine in Florence. Most now comes in ordinary bottles – the traditional straw-covered flask (*fiasco*) is more often seen hanging from walls or decorating ceilings in restaurants. Finally, if you are partial to grappa, the **Grappa di Vinacce** from Villa Calcinaia, made from the dregs of Chianti grapes, is especially well regarded. Suave and fragrant, it can easily beguile. Don't overdo it though – grappa produces terrible hangovers!

• **Cantinetta Antinori** *Pza Antinori 3; ℂ 055 292234;* 🚌 *buses 6, 11, 31 and 37; open: Mon–Fri 1200–1430, 1900–2300; reservations recommended; all credit cards accepted; Tuscan-Italian;* ❻❻-❻❻❻. When you see the church (S. Gaetano) you know you're nearly there. This smart eatery, owned by the Antinori family and located in their splendid Florentine *palazzo*, is perfect for that special occasion. The food is grown on the estate farm and, as you'd expect, the cuisine is resolutely Tuscan, featuring traditional dishes such as *bruschetta con cavolo nero* (with black cabbage) and *arista in crosta* (loin of pork). But it's the Antinori wines, famous throughout the world, which will make the meal memorable.

> **A good Chianti is bright ruby in colour and full-bodied with a strong bouquet.**

• **Enoteca Pinchiorri** *V. Ghibellina 87; ℂ 055 242777;* 🚌 *bus 14; open: Tue–Sat 1230–1330, 1930–2200, closed Wed lunch; reservations essential; all credit cards accepted; Tuscan;* ❻❻❻. Pinchiorri is first and formost a wine bar, boasting one of the best-stocked cellars in Europe. The setting is palatial – the restaurant lies to the right of a splendid courtyard adorned with

▲ Chianti vines near Panzano

palms and other greenery. When you order here, you can opt for the *menù degustazione* (sampling menu) with wine served by the glass as recommended for each dish. Note that a full meal with wine is likely to set you back considerably, since Pinchiorri won first place in the most recent *Firenze Spettacolo* survey and, more tellingly, was third in the league table of Italy's foremost wine magazine, *Civiltà del Bere*. Summer garden.

• **Magazzino Toscano** *V. dei Magazzini 2–4r;* 🚌 *bus B; open: Mon–Sat 1000–2000.* On the corner of Piazza della Signoria is this delightful store, dedicated to nothing less than the Tuscan way of life. First and foremost however, it's a wine emporium, with a wonderful selection of Chianti Classico, Tuscan, Montalcino and other Italian regional wines, champagnes and grappas. Tastings are available, accompanied by a selection of Tuscan breads and *antipasti*. You can also buy olive oils and locally produced tableware.

Piazza della Signoria

This area incorporates much of Renaissance Florence, including the Palazzo Vecchio, Florence's magnificent town hall, and the Uffizi Gallery. One of the most picturesque streets to eat in is Borgo Santi Apostoli where many medieval houses survive.

PIAZZA DELLA SIGNORIA
Restaurants

Antico Fattore ❶

V. Lambertesca 1–3r

✆ 055 288975

🚍 Bus B

Open: Mon–Sat 1215–1500, 1915–2230

Reservations recommended

All credit cards accepted

Tuscan-Italian

€ €

A quaint old-fashioned trattoria with formal but friendly service. If you don't know Italian, you can select from the English language menu. The most unusual of the Tuscan dishes is grilled pigeon.

Le Arti ❷

V. dei Neri 57r

✆ 055 288951

🚍 Bus B

Open: Tue–Sun 1200–1430, 1900–2300

Reservations recommended

All credit cards accepted

Tuscan

€ €

A formal *ristorante* with painterly décor, tucked away behind the Ponte Vecchio. There's an English language menu, which you'll appreciate when you see just what's on offer. The inventive dishes include duck with aromatic fennel and sweet wine, half pigeon with white wine sauce, slices of goose breast with pistachios, salted cod with potatoes, and T-bone steak for two people. The starters include Tuscan bread soup with black cabbage, courgette pie with béchamel sauce and bacon with rosemary and parmesan cheese.

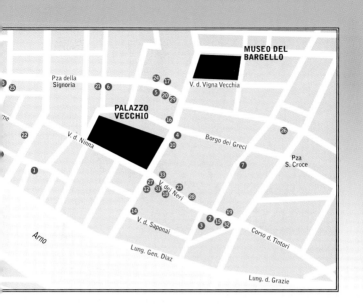

▲ Piazza della Signoria

Benvenuto

V. Mosca 16r

✆ 055 214833

🚌 Bus B

Open: Mon–Sat 1200–1430, 1900–2230

Reservations recommended

All credit cards accepted

Tuscan

€

This is a family-run trattoria, near the Arno embankment. The *casalinga* dishes are based on the home-grown produce of the owner's vegetable garden. On Fridays, opt for the *baccalà* (stockfish); otherwise try the house speciality, *cappellacci al tartufo* (a delicious pasta dish with truffle sauce) or the *scaloppina Benvenuto*. For starters try the *affetati misti* (cold meats) or the *gnocchi* (dumplings).

Buzzino ❹

V. dei Leoni 8r

✆ 055 2398013

🚌 Bus 23

Open: Tue–Sun 1200–1500, 1900–2300

Reservations unnecessary

All credit cards accepted

Tuscan-International

€€

Handy for the Uffizi, the laid-back, friendly atmosphere of Giuseppe Angeli's restaurant is its strong point. Of the Florentine dishes, try the *pappardelle alla lepre* (pasta with minced hare) followed by *cinghiale alla Maremmana* (wild boar). If you're lucky the patron will hand round the bottle of Amaro (herbal liqueur) before you leave.

Il Cantastorie ❺

V. Condotta 7/9r

✆ 055 239 6804

🚌 Bus A

Open: Wed–Mon

Reservations recommended

All credit cards accepted

Tuscan

€€

If you're a fan of Tuscan home cooking, Il Cantastorie is definitely for you. The dining area is large and spacious, the ambience relaxed and the quality of food excellent, because they do what they know best. The menu includes traditional favourites such as *pappa al pomodoro*, *ribollita*, and ravioli with truffles, with the likes of *bistecca alla fiorentina* to follow. Fish dishes are available if you let them know in advance.

Il Cavallino ❻

Pza della Signoria, corner of V. delle Farine

✆ 055 215818

🚌 Bus A

Open: daily 1100–1500, 1900–2400

Reservations recommended

All credit cards accepted

Tuscan-Italian

€€

A smart *ristorante* with outside seating over-looking the square. There are five fixed price lunch menus with two to three courses to choose from, as well as a special Tuscan menu where you get the full works, starting with *ribollita* (vegetable broth), then *bistecca alla fiorentina* (beef-steak), with *cantuccini* (biscuits) and a glass of Vin Santo to finish.

Exe Club 🕖

Volta dei Peruzzi 3r
✆ 055 217919
🚊 Bus B
Open: daily 2000–0500
Reservations recommended
All credit cards accepted
Italian
❶❷❸

This fashionable late-night eatery, in the vicinity of Santa Croce, stays open almost until dawn. Most guests begin with an aperitif or a glass of *sangria* while choosing from the range of salads. The menu changes almost every week; look out for the risotto with courgette flowers – the beef fillet with *porcini* mushrooms is also good.

La Grotta Guelfa 🕗

V. Pellicceria 5r
✆ 055 210042
🚊 Bus A
Open: Mon–Sat 1100–1500, 1900–2400
Reservations recommended
All credit cards accepted
Tuscan
❶❷❸

A large, formal restaurant with outside seating and an impressive arcaded entrance, named after one of the medieval political factions that bedevilled Florentine politics. The Tuscan gastronomic tradition is taken seriously here, and the chef's research forays have born fruit in some interesting dishes, for example *Degli Infangati* (thin noodles with *porcini* mushrooms and lard), young goat in herbs and *ossobuco* (marrowbone stewed in a pot). There's a special menu for vegetarians.

▲ Roberto

Al lume di candela ⑨

V. delle Terme 23r

✆ 055 294566

🚌 Bus B

Open: Mon–Sat 1200–1430, 1900–0200, closed Mon am

Reservations recommended

All credit cards accepted

Italian

⓿⓿

This restaurant has been around for more than half a century and, as the name suggests, is geared towards romantic candlelit dinners. It's one of the most reliable restaurants for fish – from cabbage roll with dried cod at the cheaper end of the scale to grilled squid, scampi, endives and wild sea bass.

Montecatini ⑩

V. dei Leoni 6r

✆ 055 284863

🚌 Bus 23

Open: Thu–Tue 1200–1500, 1900–2230

Reservations recommended

💳 💳 American Express

Tuscan

⓿⓿

Popular with locals, this busy trattoria at the back of the Palazzo Vecchio has a warm feel but may prove a trial to non-smokers. The fixed price menu includes baked lasagne, while the pick of the *secondi* is *cinghiale alla Toscana* (wild boar).

La Posterula ⑪

Pza Davanzati 3r

✆ 055 2381958

🚌 Bus A

Open: daily 1200–1430, 1900–2300

Reservations recommended

All credit cards accepted

Italian

⓿⓿

Quiet restaurant near the main post office and unusual because of the number of fish dishes, including a soup, grilled shrimps, scampi with curry sauce, mixed grilled fish, sole, and so on. If you're not a fish lover, there are around 20 pizza toppings to choose from.

Roberto ⑫

V. dei Castellani 4r

✆ 055 218822

🚌 Bus 23

Open: Thu–Tue 1100–1500, 1900–2400

Reservations unnecessary

All credit cards accepted

Italian

⓿⓿

This traditional trattoria, next to the Uffizi and only a few steps away from the Arno, specialises in fish dishes including smoked salmon, but also has grilled meats and pizzas. The mussel and clam soup (*zuppa di cozze e vongole*) makes a good starter.

Totò ⑬

Borgo Santi Apostoli 6r

✆ 055 212096

🚌 Bus B

Open: Thu–Tue 1200–1500, 1900–2300

Reservations recommended

All credit cards accepted

Tuscan

⓿⓿

In the heart of a historic medieval suburb (Borgo Santi Apostoli), this traditional Tuscan eatery majors in meats grilled over an open fire (*alla brace*). It's as good as place as any therefore to try *bistecca alla fiorentina* or *lombatine di vitello* (veal escalopes cooked in the frying pan) or you could opt for the buttered sole or mixed fried fish. There's a salad bar too – an unusual feature in a Florentine restaurant.

Uffizi ⑭

V. dei Castellani 22

✆ 055 219520

🚌 Bus 23

Open: Tue–Sun 1200–1430, 1900–2300

Reservations unnecessary

All credit cards accepted

Tuscan-International

⓿⓿

Handily situated for art lovers, the Uffizi has an extensive à la carte menu as well as a special tourist menu. Traditional Tuscan dishes such as *trippa alla fiorentina* (tripe in tomato sauce) and beefsteak appear alongside grilled pork chop, cheese omelette, skewer of jumbo shrimp, mixed fried seafood and 'trout dello chef'.

PIAZZA DELLA SIGNORIA
Bars, cafés and pubs

All' Antico Vinaio

V. dei Neri 65r

✆ None available

🚌 Bus B

Open: daily 1100–2100

❸

A very small traditional *mescita* (wine shop), where you can enjoy a glass of Chianti and a cheese or salami roll.

Café Gondi ⓰

V. de' Gondi 2

✆ 055 219633

🚌 Bus 23

Open: daily 0800–2200

❸

Situated on the corner of Piazza San Firenze, the café occupies part of the Palazzo Gondi, designed by Giuliano da Sangallo in 1489 (note the rusticated stone work). Enter through the huge wooden doors, take a seat at one of the marble tables and wait to be served with drinks – the hot chocolate here is delicious – sandwiches and bowls of salad.

Caffè Italiano ⓱

V. Condotta 56r

✆ 055 291082

🚌 Bus A

Open: Mon–Sat 0800–2030, 2130–2400

❸

This stately, old-fashioned café with well-stocked wooden cabinets and wrought iron chairs is best known for its own produce – coffee, tea, wines and liqueurs. It's also open for snack lunches while the choice of foreign coffees includes Arab and Bolivian.

Fiaschetteria Vecchio Casentino ⓲

V. dei Neri 17r

✆ 055 217411

🚌 Bus B

Open: Tue–Sun 1200–2100

❸–❸❸

An excellent lunch stop, especially in the winter when you can fill up on traditional Tuscan *primi piatti*, including *ribollita* and other nourishing fare. If you don't want a meal, you can sit at the bar with a glass of Chianti and a bread roll (fillings include

▲ Caffè Italiano

mortadella (salted pork), *Wurzel* and *Speck* (salamis).

Giuliano Centro 19

V. dei Neri 74r	
⊘ None available	
🔊 Bus B	
Open: Tue–Sun 0800–1500, 1700–2100, closed Sun pm	
€	

This up-market *rosticce-ria* rustles up not only roast chicken, but pasta dishes, roast potatoes and fried polenta (maize porridge). Comfortable seating.

Osteria 20

V. dei Magazzini 3	
⊘ 055 293045	
🔊 Bus A	
Open: Tue–Sun 1000–2200	
€€	

One of the last traditional hostelries in the town centre, this humble wine bar with plain wooden tables has an excellent choice of regional wines (red and white), including the very fine Nobile di Montepulciano. You can also enjoy a simple lunch of toasted bread, salami and cheese, and the *ribollita* (vegetable soup) is also good.

Perseo 21

Pza della Signoria, corner of V. dei Calzaiuoli	
⊘ None available	
🔊 Bus A	
Open: Mon–Sat 0730–2000 (until 2400 in summer)	
€	

An elegant *gelateria* with a good choice of ice creams and also rolls and sandwiches. In summer the well-dressed clientele likes to sun itself at the outside tables.

Queen Victoria 22

V. Porta S. Maria 32r	
⊘ 055 295162	
🔊 Bus B	
Open: daily 0800–2230	
€–€€	

Comfortable self-service restaurant on the street leading to the Ponte Vecchio. You could make do with a filled roll, but you'll probably be tempted by the appetising fresh salads – ready-served or you can mix your own.

Snack Bar 23

V. dei Neri 12	
⊘ None available	
🔊 Bus B	
Open: Mon–Sat 0630–2000	
€	

Handy at lunchtime if you're in the middle of sightseeing and happy to grab a sandwich (or pastry). In hot weather the fresh orange juice, milkshakes and iced tea go down a treat.

Trattoria Gabriello 24

V. Condotta 54r	
⊘ 055 212098	
🔊 Bus A	
Open: daily 1200–1430, 1900–2230	
€	

A typical downtown eatery behind Piazza della Signoria. Most of the dishes are Tuscan standards such as *ribollita* (vegetable broth), *trippa alla fiorentina* (tripe cooked in tomatoes) and *ossobuco* (veal stew in tomato sauce).

Tripe stall 25

Loggia del Porcellino	
⊘ None available	
🔊 Bus A	
Open: Mon–Sat 0900–1900	
€	

After following the custom of patting the nose of Il Porcellino (the wild boar statue in the Mercato Nuovo), stop for a traditional *lampredotto* (offal) sandwich or tripe salad at the stall. In the winter you can buy small dishes of stew as well.

Vini 26

V. dell' Anguillara 1	
⊘ None available	
🔊 Bus 23	
Open: daily 1100–2000	
€	

A tiny *mescita* (old-fashioned wine shop) so small in fact that there's standing room for only one or two people at a time. If you can squeeze in, they have a good choice of Chianti Classico.

PIAZZA DELLA SIGNORIA
Shops, markets and picnic sites

Bakeries,
confectioners and
pasta shops

Panetteria ㉗

V. dei Neri 5r

🚌 Bus B

Open: daily 0730–2000

A baker's selling traditional Florentine coarse bread as well as other fresh bread and pastries.

Ruggini ㉘

V. dei Neri 26

🚌 Bus B

Open: Tue–Sun 0730–2000

A delectable cake shop where you'll find local specialities including *schiacciata alla fiorentina* (iced sponge cake) and *bomboloni* (doughnuts, delivered hot at 1630).

Delicatessens and
grocers

Consorzio Agrario Firenze ㉙

V. Condotta 5

🚌 Bus 23

Open: daily 0800–1930

This is an important emporium for produce from the Tuscan countryside, including pecorino and other cheeses, salami, pesto, Chianti Classico wines and virgin olive oils.

Gastronomia Tassini ㉚

Borgo Santi Apostoli 24r

🚌 Bus B

Open: Mon–Sat 0800–2000, closed Wed pm

Tassini is one of the oldest delicatessens in town, with a wonderful choice of cheeses and salami, pâté, salmon mousse and ready-made dishes including fish and seafood pancakes and truffle *raviolini*.

Giuliano ㉛

V. dei Neri 5r

🚌 Bus B

Open: daily 0800–2000

Modern delicatessen with some provisions. Take a ticket from the machine by the door for your place in the queue.

Lanzo Caffè ㉜

V. dei Neri 69

🚌 Bus B

Open: daily 0800–1300, 1630–1930

Coffee specialists with a wide variety for sale; also tea, marmalade, oil, fruit in syrup, nuts and alcoholic drinks including champagne and lemon liqueur.

Primi ㉝

V. dei Neri 12

🚌 Bus B

Open: daily 0730–2000

It's a tight squeeze to get into this colourful fruit and vegetable store, where you can also buy dried pasta and truffles in oil, among other things.

Wines and oils

Gambi Romano ㉞

Borgo Santi Apostoli 21–3r and also V. Senese 21r

🚌 Bus B

Open: daily 0900–2000

Wines from around the world, champagnes, extra virgin olive oil, biscuits (*biscotti di Prato*) and the best Italian chocolates – you'll find them all here.

▲ Consorzio Agrario Firenze

Fast food

Eating on the hoof

While the pizza is a Neapolitan invention, the Florentines too have taken it to their hearts. Apart from the ubiquitous pizzeria, look out for the *rosticceria*, specialising in roast chicken and the *pasticceria* (pastries, salads, burgers, and so on).

- **Cantinetta** *V. del Proconsolo 39r;* ✆ *055 211766;* ⏺ *bus 15; open: daily 1100–2400;* ⏺. Also known as the 'Yellow Bar', Cantinetta is a convenient lunch stop for visitors to the Duomo or the Palazzo Vecchio. Pizzas are the stock in trade, with the usual range of toppings.
- **Ciao Bella** *Pza del Tiratoio 1r;* ✆ *055 218477;* ⏺ *buses 6 and D; open: Wed–Mon 1200–1500, 2000–0100;* ⏺⏺. Located in the picturesquely down-at-heel San Frediano neighbourhood, this eatery is especially popular for its pizzas and fresh fish dishes, cooked in a wood-fuelled oven. Something else to look forward to are the homemade desserts.
- **Esedra** *V. Borgo S. Frediano 44r;* ✆ *none available;* ⏺ *buses 6 and D; open: daily 1130–1500, 1830–2300, closed Mon am;* ⏺. A cheap and cheerful pizza joint in the Oltrarno, featuring Arab dishes (*shish* kebab, *falafel* and, the house speciality, 'spaghetti Ali Baba'). There's a fixed price menu at lunchtimes – if you're eating here in the evening, you could finish with a cocktail in the bar next door.
- **La Greppia** *Lung. Francesco Ferrucci 4–8;* ✆ *055 6812341;* ⏺ *bus 8; open: Tue–Sun 1200–0200;* ⏺. The late opening times make this pizzeria ideally suited to night owls reluctant to return home to their beds. During the

▲ La Greppia

day the location on the Ferrucci embankment offers pleasing views across the Arno.

• **Maioli** *V. Guicciardini 43;* ✆ *none available;*  *bus D; open: daily 0800–2000;* ❶–❶❶. Café-*pasticceria* where you can call in for a coffee and *schiacciata alla fiorentina* (iced sponge cake), or linger over lunch: *bistecca*, burgers, pizzas, pasta dishes and seafood salad are all available. Handy for the Pitti Palace.

• **Il Pizzaiuolo** *V. dei Macci 113r;* ✆ *055 241171;*  *bus 14; open: Mon–Sat 1200–1430, 1900–2400;* ❶–❶❶. As the pizza was invented in Naples and this pizzeria is owned by a Neapolitan, this is the closest you're going to get to the real thing in Florence. Consequently, booking is a must, especially as there isn't much room. Pseudo-rustic ambience.

• **Pop Corn** *V. Anton Francesco Doni 43–5;* ✆ *055 350696;*  *bus 2; open: 1200–1430, 1930–0100;* ❶. This newly renovated pizzeria has some of the lowest prices in town – especially good value as they're baked in wood-fired ovens. Draught beers are available as well as a wide selection of wines and there are theme evenings and live music.

• **Ramraj** *V. Ghibellina 61r;* ✆ *055 240999;*  *bus 14; open: Tue–Sun 1100–1330, 1700–2300 (until Fri–Sat);* ❶. This busy Indian takeaway and rotisserie, located on one of the busiest restaurant streets in the city, is much in demand with office workers in a hurry and tourists with a busy sightseeing schedule. The tandoori and other Mughal specialities include tasty Indian breads stuffed with meat or vegetables.

> **... much in demand with office workers in a hurry and tourists with a busy sightseeing schedule ...**

• **Spera** *V. della Cernaia 9r;* ✆ *055 495286;*  *bus 12; open: Sun, Tue–Fri 1000–1400, 1800–2400, closed Sun am;* ❶. A popular pizzeria, owned by a former amateur boxer, Spera produces excellent pizzas as well as an interesting range of *antipasti* including vegetarian and seafood options. There's a fixed price menu at lunchtime.

• **Yang Yang** *V. Ghibellina 60;* ✆ *none available;*  *bus 14; open: daily 1000–2000;* ❶. Chinese takeaway and *rosticceria* selling fried chicken, rice and noodle dishes.

San Lorenzo

This area bears the indelible imprint of Florence's most illustrious
mercantile dynasty, the Medici – their mausoleum lies in the church
of San Lorenzo. The local trattorias specialise in 'cucina casalinga' (home
cooking), ordering the freshest farm produce from the market right on
their doorstep.

SAN LORENZO
Restaurants

Angiolino ❶

V. Guelfa 138r

✆ 055 475292

🚍 Buses 7, 10, 11, 25, 31 and 32

Open: Fri–Wed 1200–1430, 1900–2300

Reservations essential

All credit cards accepted

Tuscan

€€–€€€

Angiolino has been a family business since 1899 and the current patron, Gian Carlo Frisella, has been in the saddle for more than a decade. Numbered among his regular clients are Florentine football heroes from the 1960s! You come here to enjoy traditional Tuscan cooking at its simple best – starters such as *gnocchetti verdi* (green dumplings), *ribollita* (vegetable broth) and wheat soup. Of the second courses, the *bistecca* (beefsteak) can be especially recommended, but save room for the tiramisu with mascarpone. Needless to say all the dishes are dressed with locally produced extra virgin olive oil (Laudemio in this case) and there's an amazing wine list – Antinori, Tignanello *et al.*

Antellesi ❷

V. Faenza 9r

✆ 055 216990

🚍 Buses 7, 10, 11, 12, 25, 31 and 32

Open: Mon–Sat 1200–1430, 1900–2230

Reservations unnecessary

💳 American Express

Tuscan

€–€€

Handy for visiting the Medici chapels, this friendly trattoria has a relaxed atmosphere and welcomes foreigners (English spoken). The steaks, served with a delicious gorgonzola sauce, are recommended and this is also a good place to try the traditional Tuscan cheese, pecorino.

Il Banchino ❸

V. dei Banchi 11–13r

✆ 055 2398790

🚍 Buses 6, 11 and A

Open: daily 1900–2300

Reservations unnecessary

All credit cards accepted

Tuscan

€€

Il Banchino is a friendly mainstream eatery with mirrored walls, close to one of Florence's most beautiful churches and squares, Santa Maria Novella. There's an English language menu to guide you through the mysteries of Tuscan cuisine – here there's a preponderance of bean and pasta dishes, while the beef fillet makes a good main course.

Hydra ❹

V. del Canto dei Nelli 38r

✆ 055 218922

🚍 Buses 1, 6, 14, 17, 22, 23, 36 and 37

Open: daily 1200–1430, 1800–2400

Reservations unnecessary

All credit cards accepted

Tuscan-Italian

€€

Hydra is bright and breezy and a useful lunch spot if you've been visiting the Medici chapels. If your Italian is not up to scratch,

▲ Palazzo Gaddi

choose from the English language menu. There's a large choice of pizzas, including fish toppings, pasta dishes, Italian standards (grilled chicken breasts, for example) and some interesting Tuscan choices, the best of which is the Tuscan wild boar with butter and sage sauce.

Lobs ⑤

V. Faenza 75r

✆ 055 212478

🚌 Buses 7, 10, 11, 12, 25, 31 and 32

Open: daily 1230–1430, 1900–2330

Reservations recommended

All credit cards accepted

Italian-Seafood

€€

The perfect antidote to too many meat courses (an occupational hazard with Tuscan cooking), Lobs deals exclusively in fish dishes and lies in the colourful market neighbourhood of San Lorenzo. The traditional *antipasti* and *primi* are dispensed with in favour of a variety of fish platters – the best introduction to what's on offer is to order the *assaggini di pesce* (fish-taster selection). Lobster tails are served with green beans or you could opt for swordfish carpaccio with melon and avocado, or octopus served on a bed of boiled potatoes. Shellfish choices include scampi and scallops. Side servings come in the form of rice and a selection of grilled or steamed vegetables. At lunch, fish is served with pasta.

Mario ⑥

V. della Rosina 2r	
✆ 055 218550	
Ⓢ Buses 1, 6, 14, 17, 22, 23, 36 and 37	
Open: Mon–Sat 1130–1500	
Reservations unnecessary	
No credit cards accepted	
Tuscan	
❻-❻❻	

A friendly trattoria near the church of San Lorenzo. The only drawback is the subtle pressure to get on with your meal so as to make way for the next shift. Enjoy the typical rustic dishes while you can!

Osteria Caterina de' Medici ⑦

Pza del Mercato Centrale 12–13r	
✆ 055 210620 (reservations)	
Ⓢ Buses 7, 10, 11, 12, 25, 31 and 32	
Open: daily 1200–1430, 1930–2300	
Reservations recommended	
💳 💳	
Tuscan-Italian	
❻❻	

A classy *ristorante* opposite the Central Market hall. You can either eat 'alla Toscana' from a menu which includes *crostini* (toasted bread with liver pâté), *ribollita* (vegetable broth) and *trippa alla fiorentina* (tripe in a piquant tomato sauce), or opt for one of the many pizza or pasta dishes.

Palazzo Gaddi (Hotel Astoria) ⑧

V. del Giglio 9	
✆ 055 2398095	
Ⓢ Buses 1, 6, 14, 17, 22, 23, 36, 37 and A	
Open: daily 1200–1430, 1800–2300	
Reservations recommended	
All credit cards accepted	
Tuscan-Italian	
❻❻❻	

A feast for the eyes, the dining rooms of this magnificent hotel restaurant date back to the Renaissance period and are decorated with frescos by Luca Giordano. The menu is extensive and might include marinated turkey with grilled artichokes, homemade crêpes stuffed with spinach, cheese and truffle cream sauce, and baked leg of veal with white wine sauce. Fish courses include baked fillet of turbot with black olives, fresh octopus salad and fresh salmon fillet. The restaurant has a terrace with a view overlooking the garden.

Palle d'Oro ⑨

V. Sant' Antonino 43/5	
✆ 055 288383	
Ⓢ Buses 7, 10, 11, 12, 25, 31 and 32	
Open: Mon–Sat 1200–1430, 1830–2145	
Reservations unnecessary	
All credit cards accepted	
Tuscan-Italian	
❻-❻❻	

Not to be confused with the Palle d'Oro in the Oltrarno, this one is handy for the Central Market. Plain cooking and unexceptional surroundings (the tables are beyond the bar), but very good value. The snacks include mozzarella cheese, *calamari* (squid), Tuscan sausage and *lampredotto* (offal).

Sabatini ⑩

V. Panzani 9/A	
✆ 055 211559	
Ⓢ Buses 6, 9 and 11	
Open: daily 1230–1445, 1930–2300	
Reservations recommended	
All credit cards accepted	

Tuscan-International

€€€

One of Florence's more exclusive restaurants, Sabatini's reputation for excellent cooking is not always deserved, especially at the prices charged. The stately ambience will appeal to traditionalists but may seem a little stuffy to the informal diner.

Il Salterona ⑪

V. Giovan Battista Zannoni 10r

☏ 055 216112

🚌 Buses 1, 6 and 17

Open: daily 1200–1500, 1900–0100

Reservations unnecessary

All credit cards accepted

Italian

€€

Decorous eatery where paintings line the walls of a long wood-panelled salon. The menu is fairly conventional with the usual combinations of chicken breast, veal steak, grilled beef, and so on, but you can also eat fish here – grilled swordfish for example or, equally appealing, shrimps stewed in lemon with cream sauce. The tourist menu is good value.

Sergio Gozzi ⑫

Pza S. Lorenzo 8r

☏ 055 281941

🚌 Buses 7, 10, 11, 12, 25, 31 and 32

Open: Mon–Sat 1200–1430 only

Reservations recommended

American Express

Tuscan

€–€€

Popular lunch spot where fish is on the menu, as well as the usual range of local dishes, cooked in the home style. Outside seating available.

Le Sorgenti ⑬

V. Chiara 6r

☏ 055 213959

🚌 Buses 7, 10, 11, 12, 25, 31 and 32

Open: Mon–Sat 1130–1430, 1900–2300

Reservations unnecessary

American Express

Chinese

€€

A taste of the orient in the heart of the Central Market. The usual range of Chinese dishes is available and there's a takeaway service if you're in a hurry.

Zà-Zà ⑭

Pza del Mercato Centrale 26r

☏ 055 215411

🚌 Buses 1, 10, 18, 19 and 25 to V. Chiara

Open: Mon–Sat 1200–1500, 1900–2300

Reservations essential

All credit cards accepted

Tuscan

€€

The quintessential trattoria, Zà-Zà is in great demand with locals and tourists alike and you may find yourself in a queue. Don't despair because the food is definitely worth the wait. You'll find all the classic Florentine dishes on the menu at very affordable prices. Home in on the *crostone* and the *salsicce e fagioli* (sausage and beans), but be sure to leave room for the honey cake (*torta di miele*).

Apollo ⑮

V. dell' Ariento 41r

✆ 055 215072

⊙ Buses 7, 10, 11, 12, 25, 31 and 32

Open: Tue–Sun 0700–2400, Sun 1700–2400

€

Instantly recognisable by the large clock behind the counter and the post-modern black-and-white décor, this nightspot is popular with zestful young Italians about to hit the disco scene. Happy hour is from 1800 to 2200 when you can make your own aperitif, or have one made up for you. There's live music from 2230 onwards – anything from techno and drum and bass to 1970s disco, funk, hip hop and R&B depending on when you happen to drop by.

The Blue Anchor ⑯

Pza del Mercato Centrale 44r

✆ 055 2654029

⊙ Buses 7, 10, 11, 12, 25, 31 and 32

Open: Wed–Mon 1100–1600, 1800–0100

€ – €€

Most tourists will be familiar with Irish bars by now, but not many will have come across a pub which offers 'traditional Scottish cuisine', for example, Inverlochy salad and smoked salmon accompanied by a glass of whisky. On Sundays this is a great stop if you're in the mood for a hearty brunch – yoghurt, cereals, scrambled eggs, or, if you're a traditionalist, roast beef and Yorkshire pudding (Scottish?!).

Bondi ⑰

V. Chiara 35r

✆ None available

⊙ Buses 7, 10, 11, 12, 25, 31 and 32

Open: daily 0700–2000

€

This place can't quite make up its mind whether it's a sandwich bar or *mescita* (wine shop). Either way it doesn't really matter, so long as you're happy with a light lunch of, for example, spaghetti *a la vongole* (clams), truffles or ham. There's wine to drink as well as coffee.

Café de Medici ⑱

V. dei Conti 20r

✆ None available

⊙ Buses 1, 6, 14, 17, 22, 23, 36 and 37

Open: daily 0800–2000

€

A modern sandwich bar with ice creams as the speciality – numerous flavours to choose from. There's an internet café next door.

Friggitoria Luisa ⑲

V. Sant' Antonino 50r

✆ 055 211636

⊙ Buses 7, 10, 11, 12, 25, 31 and 32

Open: 0730–1900

€

One of only a few 'deep fry' shops left in Florence, where you can still buy *cenci* (batter fritters), polenta (maize fritters), potato croquettes, *bomboloni* (doughnuts), and *ciambelle* (ring-shaped cakes).

Garibaldi ⑳

Pza del Mercato Centrale 34

✆ None available

⊙ Buses 7, 10, 11, 12, 25, 31 and 32

BISTRO · BAR
THE BLUE ANCHOR

Traditional Scottish Cuisine

Piazza del Mercato Centrale, 44r.
50123 FIRENZE
Tel. 055.26.54.029

▲ *Prosecco*

Open: daily 1200–1430, 1900–2230

€

This humble trattoria caters mainly for the traders in the Central Market, but it's as good a place as any to try *cucina casalinga* (homely Tuscan fare).

Pinoteca ㉑

V. dell' Ariento 47r

∅ None available

🚍 Buses 7, 10, 11, 12, 25, 31 and 32

Open: Mon–Sat 1100–2330

€

You can either eat in or take away from this Greek snack bar, serving *gyros*, kebabs, *falafel*, moussaka, Greek salads, *baklava*, and so on.

Pizzeria a Taglio ㉒

V. del Canto dei Nelli 14r

∅ None available

🚍 Buses 1, 6, 14, 17, 22, 23, 36 and 37

Open: daily 1100–2300

€

As the name implies, this fairly ordinary café specialises in pizza slices, to eat in or take away. Handy for a snack lunch if you're in the vicinity of San Lorenzo.

San Lorenzo ㉓

V. del Giglio 28r

∅ 055 289694

🚍 Buses 7, 10, 11, 12, 25, 31 and 32

Open: 1200–1430, 1900–2400

€ €

This pleasant *osteria*, is a useful lunch stop for vegetarians in particular: there's a choice of salads, omelettes (including artichokes, spinach, cheese), as well as more than 20 pizza toppings. Comfortable dining area with unfussy décor.

Snack Bar ㉔

V. dei Cerretani 12

∅ None available

🚍 Buses 1, 6. 14, 17, 22, 23, 36, 37 and A

Open: daily 0800–2200

€

A basic sandwich joint, turning out the usual mixture of filled rolls and pastries, plus salads. If the counter is packed, there are tables upstairs.

Zanobini ㉕

V. Sant' Antonino 47r

∅ 055 2396850

🚍 Buses 7, 10, 11, 12, 25, 31 and 32

Open: daily, closed Sun and Wed

€

Great on atmosphere, this raucous *mescita* has been in the hands of the present owners since the Second World War, but there has been a wine shop on the site since the 14th century when it was a focus of the *ciompi* (wool-carders) revolt. Zanobini sells its own brands of wine and olive oil as well as those of other favoured suppliers. You must book in the evenings.

SAN LORENZO
Shops, markets and picnic sites

Bakeries,
confectioners and
pasta shops

Bocca Dolce 26

V. Sant' Antonino 8r

🚌 Buses 7, 10, 11, 12, 25,
31 and 32

Open: daily 0800–1300,
1500–1900

The speciality of this
confectioners is *ferri
vecchi* – chocolate
shaped to look like iron
pliers, locks, and so on.

Panetteria 27

V. dell' Ariento 23

🚌 Buses 7, 10, 11, 12, 25,
31 and 32

Open: daily 0800–200

Freshly baked Tuscan
bread is the main item
on sale here.

Delicatessens and
grocers

Casa del Formaggio 28

V. Sant' Antonino 12

🚌 Buses 7, 10, 11, 12, 25,
31 and 32

Open: daily 0800–1300,
1600–2000

The 'House of Cheese' is
good on Italian regional
varieties such as
*pugliese, gran padano,
campagna, ricotta con
peperoncino*, and so on.

Cherubino 29

V. Sant' Antonino 8

🚌 Buses 7, 10, 11, 12, 25,
31 and 32

Open: daily 0800–1300,
1600–2000

This shop, just down
the street from a
charming candlelit
chapel dating from
1646 (*tabernacolo di
Sant' Antonino*), sells
general provisions
including cheeses and
gift-wrapped *cantuccini*.

Stenio 30

V. Sant' Antonino 49r

🚌 Buses 7, 10, 11, 12, 25,
31 and 32

Open: daily 0730–1300,
1600–2000

There are several coun-
ters in this *salumeria*:
butchers, delicatessen
and fish. Among the
items on sale are salami,
dried beans, lentils, rice,
maize, jars of huge
olives and *filetti di baccalà* (cod fillets).

Markets

Mercato Centrale 31

Pza del Mercato Centrale

🚌 Buses 7, 10, 11, 12, 25,
31 and 32

Open: Mon–Fri 0700–1400
(food halls)

This enormous steel-
and-glass structure
dates from the late 19th
century. There are two
floors. Downstairs
you'll find the meat,
fish, bread and dairy
counters. Look out for
the numerous dips and
sauces (olive mousse,
ham, truffles, *porcini*
mushroom, and so on),
mountains of cheese,
poultry and organic
foods (wines, olives,
cheeses, yoghurts,
pastas). Upstairs is a
cornucopia of fruit
and vegetables of
every description,
stretching into the
distance.

▲ Mercato Centrale

International restaurants

Fed up with pizza and pasta?

While Florentines remain stubbornly loyal to the national cuisine – and who can blame them – the following selection represents some of the alternative cooking traditions on offer.

• **Amon** *V. Palazzuolo 26–8r; ✆ 055 293146; Ⓟ buses 6, 11, 36, 37 and A; open: Mon–Sat 1200–1500, 1800–2300; reservations unnecessary; no credit cards accepted; Egyptian;* ❶-❶❶. One of a growing number of eateries in Florence specialising in Arab and Egyptian cuisine. Cheap and cheerful, but this is *the* place to sample pitta bread, which comes out of the oven twice daily, or *falafels* (spicy chickpea and vegetable croquettes). More unusual is *shauerma* (roast veal). If you have a sweet tooth, you'll also want to try the *baklavas* (filo pastry with almonds, pistachio and honey).

• **Ashoka** *V. Pisana 86r; ✆ 055 224446; Ⓟ bus 6; open: Tue–Sun; reservations unnecessary;* ▨; *Indian;* ❶❶. This restaurant in the neighbourhood of San Frediano is now expanding – a sure sign of popularity. While the sauces are a little on the mild side (adapted presumably to suit

the Florentine palate) the oriental spices and tangy flavours make a welcome change from Tuscan cuisine. The biryanis and other tandoori dishes are prepared in the traditional terracotta oven, while the vegetable naan breads and basmati rice have just the right aroma.

• **Café Caracòl** *V. dei Ginori 10r; ✆ 055 211427; Ⓟ buses 1, 6 and 17; open: Tue–Sun 1700–0200; reservations recommended; all credit cards accepted; Mexican;* ❶❶. This lively Mexican eatery, where the bar is the central feature, has recently celebrated its tenth anniversary. It's run by an Italian, though you wouldn't think so from the Latino cuisine of tacos, *fajitas*, burritos, *quesadillas*, and so on. The pick of the main courses is the Mexican paella called *veracruzana* (rice with chicken, pork, shellfish and vegetables) or you could try the *caracol*, the spicy house speciality.

• **Il Mandarino** *V. Condotta 17r; ✆ 055 2396130; Ⓟ bus A; open: Tue–Sun1200–1430, 1900–2300; reservations recommended; all credit cards accepted; Chinese;* ❶❶. This busy, unpretentious

... fast becoming a home-from-home for the many Japanese visitors to Florence ...

restaurant in the heart of the city's medieval quarter, is much frequented by the local Chinese community – always a good sign. If you're intending to head here for lunch and haven't booked, make sure you come early. The tourist menu is good value and delivered promptly, ideal for those with a tight schedule.

• **Masa** *Borgo Ognissanti 1r; ✆ 055 290978;* 🚍 *bus 12; open: daily 1930–2230; reservations essential; all credit cards accepted; Japanese;* ❶❷❸. Fast becoming a home-from-home for the many Japanese visitors to Florence, this up-market eatery in one of Florence's more historic streets specialises in the traditional 'Kaiseki' cuisine. Come prepared to relax and take your time – the chef is a perfectionist and will not be hurried.

• **Ramses** *Borgo Tegolaio 17/21r; ✆ 055 295054;* 🚍 *buses 11, 36 and 37; open: daily 1200–1500, 1900–2300; reservations recommended; all credit cards accepted; Egyptian;* ❶❷. One of the reasons why Middle-Eastern cooking is catching on in Florence is because it's such good value for money and, in this regard, Ramses continues to set the pace. *Falafels* (spicy chickpea fritters, flavoured with onion, parsley, cumin and garlic) get the tastebuds into gear, or there's houmous (*tahina* paste mixed with chickpeas, garlic and sesame paste), rice and spiced meat, or soup. The main courses include *shish* kebab (grilled roast lamb on a skewer), or an equally tasty *kofte* (grilled minced meat with onions).

• **Ruth's** *V. Carlo Farini 2a; ✆ 055 2480888;* 🚍 *bus 6; open:*

▲ Plate of *tapas*

daily 1200–1430, 1930–2300, closed Fri pm and Sat am; reservations unnecessary; all credit cards accepted; Kosher-Vegetarian; ❶–❶❷. You can detect all kinds of Arab and Middle-Eastern influences at Ruth's, although the kosher tradition is the point of departure. Daytime specialities include pitta bread with falafel and vegetables, hot salmon bagels and Tunisian couscous. In the evening there's a broth made with chickpeas and unleavened bread, fish couscous and a delicious fried pasta dish.

• **Salamanca** *V. Ghibellina 80r; ✆ 055 2345452;* 🚍 *bus 14; open: daily 1930–0200; reservations recommended;* 🔲*; Spanish;* ❶–❶❷. This buzzing *tapas* bar and restaurant with attractive, pseudo-Spanish décor is a great place to meet people and make friends. The menu is pretty much what you would expect: *tostadas*, *bocadillos*, cheese and ham platters, salads, soups, fish and paella. If there are two of you, try the *verbenas*, a taster platter comprising a mixture of *tapas*. To drink there's a selection of Spanish beers and wines and on Monday evenings you can look forward to live performances by Latin-American artists.

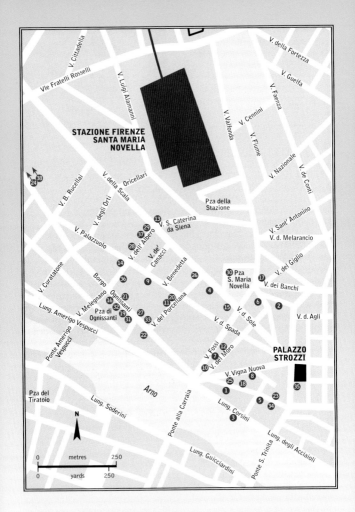

Santa Maria Novella

The main artery of this central district is Borgo Ognissanti, an elegant
street of handsome palaces and attractive shops, including several
inviting delicatessens. The word 'borgo' implies that in medieval times
this was a hamlet outside the city walls.

SANTA MARIA NOVELLA
Restaurants

Il Barretto ❶

V. del Parione 50r

☎ 055 294122

🚌 Buses A and B

Open: Mon–Sat 1200–1500, 1900–2300

Reservations unnecessary

All credit cards accepted

Italian

€€

Though a little stuffy for some tastes, with a rather formal dining space, Il Barretto concentrates on a small selection of simple but appetising dishes – veal liver with sage for example, or diced chicken breast served with black olives. Save room for the homemade cakes and desserts, any of which can be recommended.

Buca Lapi ❷

V. del Trebbio 1r

☎ 055 213768

🚌 Bus 11

Open: Mon–Sat 1230–1430, 1930–2230

Reservations recommended

All credit cards accepted

Tuscan-Italian

€€€

Well known to locals, this cellar restaurant dates back to the 1880s. Somewhat lacking in atmosphere, unusual Tuscan specialities provide the main draw.

Try the pan-fried tripe (*tegamino di trippa alla fiorentina*).

Città di Firenze ❸

Lung. Corsini 4

☎ 055 217706

🚌 Buses 3 and 15

Open: Tue–Sun 1230–1430, 1900–0100

Reservations unnecessary

All credit cards accepted

Italian-International

€€

This elegant wine bar-restaurant is pleasantly situated on the Arno embankment. Its main claim to fame is that it was once the home of Louis Bonaparte, King of Holland. Though it seems to appeal primarily to a well-heeled clientele, it's not as expensive as it looks providing you choose carefully from the menu. The musical accompaniment is live piano or classical.

Il Coccodrillo ❹

V. della Scala 5

☎ 055 283622 or 055 218355 (for bookings)

🚌 Buses 6, 11, 12, 36, 37 and A

Open: daily 1230–1530, 1900–2230

Reservations recommended

All credit cards accepted

Tuscan

€€

Lunchtime specialities in this typical downtown restaurant include *crostini*, chicken breast and pork cutlet. Evening diners choose from the à la carte menu; late-night snacks are available from the piano bar after 2230.

Coco Lezzone ❺

V. del Parioncino 26r

☎ 055 287178

🚌 Buses A and B

Open: Mon–Sat 1200–1430, 1900–2200

Reservations recommended

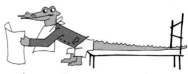

ristorante il coccodrillo

Via della Scala, 5 - Tel. 055/283.622 - FIRENZE

No credit cards accepted

Tuscan

Highly regarded by local 'foodies', this restaurant was patronised by Prince Charles on a visit to Florence (there are photographs on the wall to prove it). It's an informal place with white tiles and red-checked table cloths and serves unassuming but wholesome Tuscan standards. Not hugely expensive and good value.

Croce al Trebbio 6

V. delle Belle Donne 47–9r

☎ 055 287089

🚍 Bus A

Open: Tue–Sun 1200–1500, 1900–2300

Reservations recommended

All credit cards accepted

Tuscan-Italian

Busy trattoria very popular with locals, especially in the evenings. As a starter, try one of the typically Florentine bread-based soups – the *ribollita* for example is a heartwarming mix of beans, cabbage, carrot and spices. The predominantly meaty main courses include a succulent *ossobuco* (knuckle of veal stew in tomato sauce). Occasional live music.

Garga 7

V. del Moro 48r

☎ 055 2398898

🚍 Bus A

Open: daily 1930–2330

Reservations recommended

All credit cards accepted

Tuscan

This fashionable bistro attracts the Florentine *beau monde* with its inventive Tuscan cooking. Worth the expense if you're looking for an excuse to celebrate. Smart dress advised.

I Latini 8

V. dei Palchetti 6r

☎ 055 210916

🚍 Bus A

Open: Tue–Sun 1230–1430, 1930–2200

Reservations recommended

💳 American Express

Tuscan

Definitely one of the best eating experiences

in Florence. This much-loved trattoria is owned by the Latini family, father and sons. It's so popular that even if you've booked, you'll end up in a queue of patient and good-humoured locals hoping for a table. To help pass the time guests are offered a glass of wine and nibbles on the house. You'll be seated elbow-to-elbow with other diners – a great opportunity to try out your Italian. The written menu, if there is one, is usually nowhere to be seen; instead the waiter rehearses the list of tried and tested Tuscan favourites, usually centring around a huge *bistecca* (beefsteak). A huge carafe of very drinkable red house wine is shared out by each table, and after dessert the meal is rounded off with Vin Santo and *biscotti di Prato*.

Osteria dei Centopoveri 9

V. Palazzuolo 31	
✆ 055 2184672	
🚌 Buses 6, 11, 12, 36, 37 and A	
Open: Mar–Oct daily 1900–2300, lunch 1230–1500	
Reservations essential	
All credit cards accepted	
Tuscan-Italian	
€€	

This easy-going local eatery attracts a mainly youthful clientele – there's a pub next door. The owners are from southern Italy which explains why, in addition to the usual range of Tuscan dishes, there's salmon and grilled fish on the menu.

Osteria N.1 10

V. del Moro 22	
✆ 055 294318	
🚌 Bus A	
Open: Mon–Sat 1200–1500, 1900–2400	
Reservations recommended	
All credit cards accepted	
Tuscan-Venetian	
€€€	

Situated in an historic neighbourhood of antique shops and artisanal premises, Gianni Girardi's stylish restaurant is ideally suited to that special occasion. Pheasant is one of the specialities of the house.

Sostanza detto 'il Troia' 11

V. del Porcellana 25r	
✆ 055 212691	
🚌 Bus 12	
Open: Mon–Fri 1200–1500, 1930–2330	
Reservations essential	
No credit cards accepted	
Tuscan	
€€	

Another place with a nickname: 'il Troia' means 'slut', a reference to the first owner, said to have had the nasty habit of laying his greasy hands on the customers. One of the few genuine trattorias left in Florence, Sostanza is a tiny establishment, celebrated for its local dishes, including artichoke pie.

La Spada 12

V. del Moro 66r	
✆ 055 218757	
🚌 Bus A	
Open: Mon–Sat 1100–1500, 1900–2400	
Reservations unnecessary	
All credit cards accepted	
Tuscan-Italian	
€€	

A bright, modern restaurant and *rosticceria* (meat roasted on a spit is the house speciality) offering plain, but nourishing fare. You can eat Tuscan with *ribollita* (vegetable broth) and *trippa alla fiorentina* (tripe) or mainstream Italian – lasagne, roast beef, pork chops, and so on.

SANTA MARIA NOVELLA
Bars, cafés and pubs

L'Angelo

V. della Scala /V. S. Caterina da Siena

☎ 055 213331

🚌 Buses 1, 2, 9, 16, 17, 22, 29, 30 and D

Open: daily 0500–2400

€

This busy corner café and bar makes an excellent breakfast stop, especially if, like many Florentines, you have a sweet tooth. The delights in store include the mouth-watering pastry *schiacciata* (usually served with fruits), crème caramel and *barchette* filled with apple and pear; also filled baguettes, *bresaola*, etc.

Il Cantuccio 🟡

V. Maso Finiguerra 19

☎ None available

🚌 Bus 12

Open: daily 0730–2300

€

Stand up café-bar, popular with students and selling *gnocchi*, crêpes and other snacks.

Chequers 🟡

V. della Scala 7r

☎ 055 287588

🚌 Buses 6, 11, 12, 36, 37 and A

Open: Tue–Sun 1800–0130 (until 0230 Fri–Sat)

€

Cavernous, English-style pub with English-speak-ing staff and a transient clientele, including many visitors. As you'd expect, there's an excellent choice of draught beers and the pub snacks include fish and chips as well as sandwiches, salads, hot-dogs and sweets. If you want to save money, the happy hour is from 2000 until 2200 (drinks half price) while the music (loud) is Indie/mainstream.

Curtatone 🟡

Borgo Ognissanti 167r

☎ 055 210772

🚌 Bus 12

Open: Wed–Mon 0700–0100

€

Located in the same block as the Hotel Argentina, this busy, popular *pasticceria* with a low brick-vaulted ceiling attracts a mainly young clientele. The mouth-watering counter displays include filled rolls, Tuscan biscuits and chocolates.

Fiddler's Elbow 🟡

Pza S. Maria Novella 7

☎ None available

🚌 Buses 6, 11, 12, 36, 37 and A

Open: daily 1300–0200

€

Small Irish pub, always full to bursting with tourists and soldiers

from the nearby barracks. The main draw is the satellite TV and of course Irish beers. There's also a comedy club, but you have to book as seats are limited.

Latte & Co

V. del Parione 46r	
✆ 055 283397	
🚌 Buses A and B	
Open: Mon–Sat 0800–2000	
💶	

A young people's hang out, this designated trattoria is really little more than a café selling filled rolls, biscuits, confectionery and fresh orange juice. The no smoking rule is a definite plus.

Il Mostrino 19

Borgo Ognissanti 59	
✆ None available	
🚌 Bus 12	
Open: Tue–Sun 1100–1500, 1900–2400	
💶💶	

Tuscan fare is the mainstay of this small, traditional eatery. The fixed price menu at lunch – three courses with a half bottle of wine or water – is good value.

Palazzo Panificio 20

V. Palazzuolo 23	
✆ None available	
🚌 Buses 6, 11, 12, 36, 37 and A	
Open: daily 0730–1300, 1630–1900	
💶	

You'll find this tempting cake shop next door to the church of San

Paolino. Beside the usual range of Italian pastries and sweetmeats, you'll see brownies, fudges, bagels and American muffins.

Piccioli 21

Borgo Ognissanti 86	
✆ None available	
🚌 Bus 12	
Open: daily 0700–2000	
💶	

A bar with a second string in pastries, cakes and biscuits, notably *biscotti alla mandorla* (almonds); you can also buy tiny, but appetising, filled rolls and croissants.

Pizzeria 22

Borgo Ognissanti 45	
✆ None available	
🚌 Bus 12	
Open: daily 1100–2200	
💶	

Useful lunch stop, not far from the station, if all you want is a quick snack. A range of toppings and a small-size pizza will not break the bank.

Rose's Café 23

V. del Parione 26r	
✆ 055 287090	
🚌 Buses A and B	
Open: Mon–Sat 0800–0100, Sun 1700–0100	
💶	

The American-style bar is a magnet for young city workers. From 1900 until 2300 it doubles as a sushi bar, serving typical Japanese specialities including *hakkimaki*, *sakkimaki* and *tempura*.

La Rotonda 24

Il Prato 10/16	
✆ 055 2654644	
🚌 Buses 1, 20, 9, 12, 16, 26, 27 and 80	
Open: daily 1000–2400	
💶	

Lively pub-bar teeming with Florentine teenagers and twenty-somethings, especially at weekends. Pizzas and other basic dishes available, when and if you can find a table.

La Vigna 25

V. Vigna Nuova 82r	
✆ None available	
🚌 Bus A	
Open: daily 0730–2000	
💶	

This bar and pastry shop (*pasticceria*) sells snacks, a choice of Tuscan breads, chocolates, sweets and nuts; also grappa.

SANTA MARIA NOVELLA
Shops, markets and picnic sites

Bakeries, confectioners and pasta shops

Dolceforte 26

V. della Scala 21

🚌 Buses 6, 11, 12, 36, 37 and A

Open: daily 1000–1300, 1530–1930

Purveyors of chocolates fashioned into weird and wonderful shapes – planes, telephones, and so on. You'll also find mouth-watering displays of marzipan, honey, marmalade and biscuits. Anything here would make a suitable gift for the non-calorie conscious.

Palatresi 27

Borgo Ognissanti 74

🚌 Bus 12

Open: daily 0730–1330, 1700–2000, closed Wed pm

Local bakery with a good line in biscuits, including *occhi di bue* (ox's eyes), as well as pasta and wines.

Panificio 28

V. dell' Albero 21 and also at V. Palazzuolo 154r

🚌 Buses 6, 11, 12, 36, 37 and A

Open: daily 0730–1330, 1430–2000

Small local bakery, selling the coarse, unsalted Florentine bread, known

as *casalingo*, also croissants and pastries.

Pasta Fresca 29

V. dell' Albero 1

🚌 Buses 6, 11, 12, 36, 37 and A

Open: daily 0830–1300, 1630–1930, closed Wed pm

As the name implies, they produce their own fresh pasta here including ravioli *di patate* and *pici* (a kind of spaghetti). Come early in the morning and you can watch the production process.

Delicatessens and grocers

Asia Masala 30

Pza S. Maria Novella 21–2r

Open: daily 0800–1300, 1600–2000, closed Mon am

🚌 Buses 6, 11, 12, 36, 37 and A

An Aladdin's cave of oriental groceries. There are more than 1 600 products in all, everything from Thai soups to Sri Lankan chilli peppers, Chinese sauces and Indian beers.

Frutteria 31

Borgo Ognissanti 49

🚌 Bus 12

Open: daily 0800–1300, 1600–1930

This fruit and vegetable shop (fresh truffles for sale) also has a range of biscuits and good value wines.

Gastronomia Braccini 32

Borgo Ognissanti 121r

🚌 Bus 12

Open: daily 0800–1300, 1600–2000

Wine shop and delicatessen with a good range of cheeses, including gorgonzola *al mascarpone* and pecorino, biscuits, *cenci*, Chianti Classico and other regional wines.

Mauro 33

Borgo Ognissanti 72

🚌 Bus 12

Open: daily 0830–1300, 1630–1930

At first sight, a common or garden butcher's, but in addition to the usual haunches of meat, you'll find displays of cooked hams and salamis – worth bearing in mind if you're thinking of a picnic.

Orizi 34

V. del Parione 19r

🚌 Buses A and B

Open: daily 0800–2000

Neighbourhood grocer's shop with a counter selling pastries and cheeses. Locals call in at lunchtimes for a bite to eat and a glass of wine.

Procacci

V. Tornabuoni 64

🚌 Buses 6, 11, 36 and 37

Open: daily 0800–2000

This opulent deli-catessen was established more than a century ago which you might guess from the marble floor and traditional wooden shelving. You can enjoy a superb sandwich at the bar-counter, washed down with a glass of Chianti.

Tripe stall 36

V. Maso Finiguerra; opposite the Hotel Adriatico

🚌 Bus 12

Open: daily 1000–2000

Panini with *lampredotto* (offal) is the speciality here! It's not to every-one's taste, but try it on a cold day served with a hot sauce.

Upac 37

V. dell' Albero 7

🚌 Buses 6, 11, 12, 36, 37 and A

Open: daily 0900–1300, 1600–2000

Useful mini-market, selling gift-wrapped *cantuccini*, *panforte* and grappa, as well as the usual grocery lines. Look out for bargains, reduced price Vin Santo for example.

Picnic sites

La Cascine 38

Parco dell Cascine, Vle Lincoln

🚌 Buses 1, 9 and 12

Open: Tue 0800–1300 (market)

If you're looking to get away from other tourists and fancy a picnic, Parco dell Cascine is just sufficiently off the beaten track. Though a little down at heel nowadays, there are enough reminders of its heyday in the 18th century, when the Florentine nobility came here to promenade and be admired by the plebs who found their own entertainment in the firework displays organised to mark public holidays. On Tuesdays there's a market here and you can buy everything from second-hand clothes to vegetables, fruit and chickens. To work off your picnic, you could take a stroll along the banks of the Arno or, if the summer heat is getting to you, there's an open-air swimming pool in the grounds of the park.

A taste of oil

'Just a drop of oil – but of course it must be extra virgin ...'

The advice above crops up all the time in Italian cookery books and you hear it with equal regularity from Florentine chefs. Everyone agrees that olive oil can make or break a dish and Tuscans are convinced that theirs is the best in the world. Oil is a **vital ingredient** in any number of traditional dishes – in *fettunta* for example where it's dribbled on to unsalted bread, or in *ribollita* and bean dishes. Typical Tuscan oils are green in colour with a glint of golden yellow; they have a herb-like aroma and a strong, highly distinctive taste. Opinion is divided over which is superior, the bitter or the fruity varieties. Every Florentine has his or her favourite and it's quite usual to drive out to a particular farm in Settignano, say, to stock up.

Olive cultivation spread to Italy from the Middle East in Roman times. When Etruria was overrun in the 4th century BC, the Romans were amazed to find an abundance of vineyards, grain fields and olive groves. During the Middle Ages the secrets of cultivation were preserved by great religious houses like the Benedictine **Monastery of Monteoliveti** (Mount of Olives) near Siena. The modern industry was revived in the Papal States during the nineteenth century.

Most of the trees used to produce Tuscan oil are at least one hundred years old and belong to the *Moraiolo*, *Frantoio* and *Leccino* varieties. Despite technological advances, leading producers still prefer to harvest the crop by hand (*brucatora*) in baskets or using a stretched cloth at the base of the plant. This avoids bruising or tearing, which can lead to rancidity. The trees flower in late spring and the tiny white flowers are of two different types; it's the ones with combined masculine and feminine characteristics that produce the fruit. **Harvesting** takes place towards the end of November – according to a local

proverb, it must be completed by the feast of Santa Lucia (13 December). Traditionally, the end of November is a time of celebration throughout the Chianti region. The day after gathering, the olives are packed and carefully transported to the *fattoria* for processing. After washing (to remove all traces of leaf or soil) they are pressed between millstones, then the thick greenish paste is given a thorough stirring to make extraction easier. No chemicals or other additives are used at any stage. Only oil with a maximum acidity of one per cent is designated *extra vergine.*

If you're thinking of taking some olive oil home with you as a souvenir, look for the black cockerel label (**Chianti Classico**) or one of the well-known brands: **Frantoio di Santa Tea** (in production since 1585), **Torciano** or **Montalcino**, for example. Tuscan oils are perfectly suited to meat soups, boiled vegetables, green beans and pasta dishes; some varieties, however, are too intrusive for making salad dressings or mayonnaise. Olive oil is of great nutritional value and an essential ingredient of the famously healthy Mediterranean diet. It is known to reduce the risk of arteriosclerosis and heart attack by driving down levels of cholesterol in the body. When frying make sure that the flame is not too high, so as not to spoil the flavour, and don't cook for longer than 20 minutes. Note that extra virgin oil should never be

Only oil with a maximum acidity of one per cent is designated 'extra vergine'.

reused and should be stored away from direct sunlight.

Extra virgin olive oil is widely available in wine shops and delicatessens, or visit the following specialist:

• **La Bottega dell' Olio** *Pza del Limbo 2r;* ✆ *055 2670468;* ◉ *bus A.* This fascinating little store stocks every conceivable variety and encourages tastings. You can ask questions in English and some literature is also available.

The best time to visit the olive groves themselves is between the end of November and the beginning of December, when you can watch the various stages of the harvesting process. Contact the **tourist office** on *055 2760381* or get in touch with the estates direct:

• Santa Tea, Reggello. ✆ *055 868117.*
• Pratomagno. ✆ *055 2340742.*

There are winter **festivals and 'oil fairs'** in Montespertoli (✆ *0571 609412*), Calenzano (✆ *055 88331*), Figline (✆ *055 951596*) and Barberino Val d' Elsa (✆ *055 80521*).

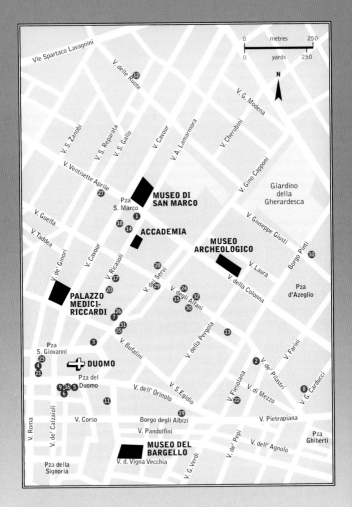

Vle Spartaco Lavagnini

metres 250
yards 250

N

V. delle Ruote 12

V. G. Modena

V. S. Zanobi
V. S. Reparata
V. S. Gallo
V. Cavour
V. A. Lamarmora
V. Cherubini

V. Ventisette Aprile
27

V. Gino Capponi

Giardino
della
Gherardesca

**MUSEO DI
SAN MARCO**

Pza
S. Marco
1

V. Guelfa
V. Taddea
V. Cavour
18
14

ACCADEMIA

V. Giuseppe Giusti

**MUSEO
ARCHEOLOGICO**

V. Laura

Borgo Pinti
10

V. de' Ginori
V. Ricasoli
28
17
29
V. de' Servi

Pza
d'Azeglio

**PALAZZO
MEDICI-
RICCARDI**

20
24
15 32
30

V. degli Alfani
V. della Colonna

26
7
31
25

13

V. della Pergola

Pza
S. Giovanni
23
4
21

3

V. Bufalini

V. de' Pilastri
2
V. Farini

✚ **DUOMO**

Pza del
Duomo

9 16 5
6

11

V. dell' Orinolo
V. S. Egidio
V. Fiesolana
V. di Mezzo
22

8
V. G. Carducci

V. Roma
V. de' Calzaioli

V. Corso

Borgo degli Albizi
V. Pandolfini
V. dell' Agnolo
V. Pietrapiana

Pza
Ghiberti

19

**MUSEO DEL
BARGELLO**

V. de' Pepi
V. G. Verdi
V. dell' Agnolo

Pza della
Signoria

V. d. Vigna Vecchia

Duomo

The squares and side streets around Brunelleschi's magnificent
cathedral are packed with restaurants and snack bars, many of them
surprisingly good value. Tourists heading for the Accademia art gallery to
see Michelangelo's *David* will encounter students from the university,
who patronise the area's cheaper bars and cafés.

DUOMO
Restaurants

Accademia ❶

Pza S. Marco 7r

☎ 055 217343

🚍 Buses 1, 6, 7, 10, 11, 17, 20, 25, 31 and 32

Open: daily 1200–1430, 1900–2230

Reservations unnecessary

All credit cards accepted

Tuscan-Italian

€–€€

A cheap and cheerful eatery, across the road from the famous art gallery, patronised largely by students. There's a choice of small and large pizzas, but it's the fresh salads that catch the eye.

Acquacotta ❷

V. de' Pilastri 51r

☎ 055 242907

🚍 Bus B

Open: Mon–Sat 1200–1430, 1900–2230

Reservations recommended

🚾

Tuscan

€–€€

Named after a popular local dish from the Maremma – thick vegetable soup with poached egg and toast – this family-run trattoria with an agreeably rustic ambience offers the usual Florentine standards at affordable prices.

Le Botteghe di Donatello ❸

Pza del Duomo 28r

☎ 055 216678

🚍 Buses 14 and 23

Open: daily 1200–2400

Reservations unnecessary

All credit cards accepted

Italian

€€

This restaurant is so close to the cathedral Baptistery that it really might have been on the site of Donatello's workshop. The atmosphere is relaxed and informal, the menu wide-ranging, everything from pizzas to fresh salads, pasta dishes and a few tempting *secondi*, for example *involtini di manzo alla Toscana* (beef roulade) or *calamari* (squid) with garlic and white wine sauce.

▲ Le Botteghe di Donatello

Buca San Giovanni ④

Pza S. Giovanni 8
✆ 055 287612
🚍 Buses 14 and 23
Open: daily 1200–1500, 1900–2400
Reservations recommended
All credit cards accepted
Tuscan-Italian
❷❸

The word *buca* means 'hole' or – interpreted more picturesquely – a cellar. This long-established *ristorante* is directly opposite the Duomo and seems to attract a youngish clientele. The menu is in English as well as Italian which may help you find your way through the Tuscan soups, mini dumplings and courgette pudding in onion sauce, followed by salmon with truffles and asparagus tips, salted cod with chickpeas, veal escalope and other grills. The pasta with baby shrimp sauce goes down well.

Il Caminetto ⑤

V. dello Studio 34r
✆ 055 2396274
🚍 Buses 14 and 23
Open: Thu–Tue 1100–1500, 1900–2400
Reservations recommended
No credit cards accepted
Tuscan
❷❸

In the shadow of the Duomo and down a little side street, Il Caminetto is an unpretentious, homely trattoria offering daily as well as à la carte menus. Tuscan soups such as *ribollita* (vegetable broth) and *pappa al pomodoro* (tomato mush), pastas, *trippa al fiorentina* (tripe with tomato sauce) and grilled meats including *bistecca* (beefsteak) are the mainstays.

Dante and Beatrice ⑥

V. delle Oche 15
✆ 055 210698
🚍 Buses 14 and 23
Open: daily 1200–1500, 1900–2330
Reservations unnecessary
All credit cards accepted
Tuscan
❷❸

The name recalls the great medieval poet, who was born not far from here, and his fictional heroine, Beatrice. The menu features the traditional Tuscan soups, bean dishes, pasta and grilled meats, including *bistecca alla fiorentina* (beefsteak). Selection of Chianti Classico and other good regional wines.

Hong Kong ⑦

V. dei Servi 35r
✆ 055 239 8235
🚍 Buses 14 and 23
Open: daily 1200–1430, 1900–2300
Reservations unnecessary
💳 American Express
Chinese
❶–❷❸

Tucked away behind the Duomo, this large Chinese restaurant is a welcome port of call for anyone looking for a change from Italian cooking. Here it's standard Cantonese, with excellent-value set menus to recommend it. The service is typically attentive.

La Libra ❽

V. G. Carducci 5

✆ 055 244794

🚍 Bus C

Open: Mon–Sat 1230–1430,
2000–2400, closed Sat am

Reservations recommended

💳 💳

Italian

€€

You'll find this culinary laboratory in a renovated warehouse across the road from the Sant' Ambrogio Market. Not the place to take a partner for a romantic dinner, La Libra appeals first and foremost to discerning diners who know their onions and are not put off by the rather tacky décor. The menu changes regularly, but features different facets of Italian regional cuisines.

Ottorino ❾

V. delle Oche 12–16r

✆ 055 218747

🚍 Buses 14 and 23

▲ Il Sasso di Dante

Open: Mon–Sat 1100–1500, 1900–2400

Reservations recommended

All credit cards accepted

Tuscan-Italian

This large, very busy *ristorante* is only a few minutes walk from the Duomo, tucked away on an attractive side street. The cuisine is resolutely Florentine with grilled meats to the fore and veal the speciality.

Relais Le Jardin 10

Hotel Regency, Pza d' Azeglio 3

✆ 055 245247

🚍 Buses 6, 31, 32 and C

Open: daily 1200–1430, 1930–2230

Reservations recommended

All credit cards accepted

Italian

The Hotel Regency served as a private residence for cabinet ministers in the mid-19th century when Florence was briefly the Italian capital. The dining room, Relais le Jardin, retains the period flavour with original furnishings, wooden wainscoting and painted glass doors. The young master chef is in fact Neapolitan; here he breathes new life into traditional Tuscan cooking, giving it a new delicacy and refinement. The *antipasti* are particularly innovative – artichoke flan with salted cod in fresh tomato sauce, for example, or timbale of crêpes with chicken liver, vegetables and truffle *velouté*. Among the *primi*, the home-made *pappardelle* with duck and broccoli sauce deserves mention; while the main courses include lamb with aromatic herbs, gorgonzola cheese ravioli and red turnips, and bundle of veal with sweetbreads and fried mushrooms on a purée of fava beans. For dessert the goats' cheese soufflé with honey and ginger sauce is recommended.

Il Sasso di Dante 11

Pza della Pallottole 6r

✆ 055 282113

🚍 Buses 14 and 23

Open: daily 1200–1430, 1900–2300

Reservations recommended

All credit cards accepted

Tuscan-Italian

Only a couple of min-utes' walk from the cathedral, Il Sasso di Dante is picturesquely set in a little square just out of sight of the Piazza del Duomo. The covered forecourt serves as a terrace and the décor includes fancy scrolling with quota-tions from Dante's masterpiece, the *Divine Comedy*. The food, while nothing out of the ordi-nary, is good value and can be relied upon.

Taverna del Bronzino 12

V. del Ruote 25r

✆ 055 495220

🚍 Buses 17, 25 and 33

Open: Mon–Sat 1200–1430, 1930–2330

Reservations recommended

All credit cards accepted

Tuscan-Italian

The former studio of the 16th-century artist, Bronzino, provides an elegant setting for this busy, laid-back restau-rant. The menu includes classic Tuscan favourites such as *crostini* with liver pâté, and fried brains with artichokes, but Bronzino is also celebrated for the inventiveness of its classical Italian cooking (all regions). Try the prawn cocktail, steaks, potato *gnocchetti* (dumplings) or fish *velouté*. Extensive wine list.

Il Teatro 13

V. degli Alfani 47r

✆ 055 2479327

🚍 Bus 15

Open: Mon–Sat 1200–1500, 1900–2300

Reservations recommended

Italian

The homely ambience and the fish specialities are the main recommen-dations of this typical trattoria. It gets lower marks for service, which is a little casual, and for some of the nouvelle cuisine dishes which tend to be overcooked. Convenient for visiting the Accademia.

DUOMO
Bars, cafés and pubs

Bar Lidia 🔟

V. Ricasoli 83r

∅ None available

🔘 Buses 6, 10, 11, 17, 20, 31, 32 and C

Open: daily 0700–2000

€

This snack bar, near the Piazza San Marco, sells the usual range of filled rolls – cheese, mozzarella, ham, tomato, and so on; also cakes.

Brunelleschi 🔟

V. degli Alfani 69r

∅ None available

🔘 Bus C

Open: daily 0800–2000

€

A pleasant spot for morning coffee, you sit at one of the outside tables in the shade of the walls of a 17th-century convent. Inside you can order from a choice of small pizzas, filled rolls, bagels or ice cream.

Coquinarius 🔟

V. delle Oche 15r

∅ 055 2302153

🔘 Buses 14 and 23

Open: Mon–Sat 0900–2400

€

You can eat in this very pleasant wine bar at any time of the day – breakfast is served at 0900 and the kitchen is

closed at 2230. As far as food is concerned, the emphasis is on snacks, although there are a number of hot and cold dishes. There's a wine cellar downstairs and tastings are available.

Gelateria Carabé 🔟

V. Ricasoli 60r

∅ 055 289476

🔘 Buses 1, 6, 11 and 17

Open: daily 0800–2000

€

One of the best ice-cream parlours in Florence, this Sicilian-run outfit near the Accademia sells delicious homemade lemon *granita* (shaved ice) as

well as traditional *gelato*. Try the *cassata siciliana* (otherwise known as tutti frutti).

Gran Café San Marco 🔟

V. Cavour 50

∅ 055 284235

🔘 Buses 1, 6, 7, 17 and 25

Open: daily 0800–2300

€–€€

This huge cafeteria and cake shop (part of the Hotel San Marco) has a garden terrace at the rear. The main seating areas are beyond the patisserie section. A variety of pizzas are sold here as well as main courses of breast

▲ Gran Café San Marco

CAFFÈ
COQUINARIUS®
WINE BAR

Degustazione vini
Piatti freddi & caldi
Spuntini & aperitivi
Dolci & gelati
Degustazione caffe & tisane
Cioccolate calde
Grandi distillati

Via delle Oche, 15 r
(traversa di via Calzaiuoli)
50122 FIRENZE
Tel. 055 23 02 153
dalle 9 fino a tarda sera
Domenica chiuso

of chicken, veal stew, Florentine pancakes, and so on. Convenient for the San Marco Convent.

The Lion's Fountain

Borgo degli Albizi 34r
✆ 055 2344412
🚌 Bus A
Open: daily 1100–0200
€

A regular port of call for Guinness lovers, this Irish bar has a typically warm, friendly atmosphere, good mainstream pop music and a range of pub grub, mainly salads and sandwiches, available till late. The other main attraction is the American football (and other sport) on TV, and of course the dart board.

Oliandolo ⑳

V. Ricasoli 38–40r
✆ 055 211296
🚌 Buses 1, 6, 11 and 17
Open: Mon–Sat 1200–1600
€

An attractive neighbourhood *mescita* (wine bar) in the vicinity of the Accademia. Open for lunch only, they sell a variety of tasty snacks and other morsels, including cheese or ham sandwiches, *crostini* (toasted bread with pâté), marinated aubergine and cheese-cake.

La Piazza ㉑

Pza S. Giovanni 25r
✆ None available
🚌 Buses 14 and 23
Open: daily 0800–2300
€

This cafeteria with tea-room (*sala da tè*) is a useful lunch stop if you've just come out of the Duomo. You'll find it in the square beside the Baptistry. The pizza slices (*pizza a taglio*) go down a treat, while there's also a choice of filled rolls. If the heat is getting to you, cool down with a milkshake.

Rex's Café ㉒

V. Fiesolana 25r
✆ 055 2480331
🚌 Bus C
Open: daily 1700–0230
€

This late-night bar, a popular meeting place for local Florentines, serves cocktails and aperitifs, and light snacks into the small hours. Occasional live entertainment. Happy hour 1700 to 2130.

Scudieri ㉓

Pza S. Giovanni 19r
✆ 055 289218
🚌 Buses 14 and 23
Open: daily 0700–2100
€

A large, old-fashioned *pasticceria* with chandeliers and wood panelling. The snacks include filled rolls and croissants, but you may find the cakes and pastries more tempting. They include *schiacciata alla fiorentina* (orange sponge), plum cake and polenta. The Italian beer Nastro Azzuro is available on draught.

Il Vinaio ㉔

V. degli Alfani
✆ None available
🚌 Bus C
Open: daily 1200–2000
€

Typical old-fashioned *fiaschetteria* with trademark tiled walls and marble top tables. Call in at lunchtime if there's room and catch up on the local gossip over a glass of Chianti and a sandwich.

Zurito ㉕

V. dei Servi 12r
✆ None available
🚌 Buses 14 and 23
Open: Mon–Sat 0700–0130
€

Small, busy *pasticceria* on the way to the Duomo. Sells cakes, pastries, biscuits, also lasagne and other oven-baked pastas.

DUOMO
Shops, markets and picnic sites

Dulcis 26

V. dei Servi 31r

🚍 Buses 14 and 23

Open: daily 0800–1300, 1500–2000

This delightful little shop is within sight of the Duomo and is well worth a browse. You'll find gift-wrapped chocolates, marzipan, mints and sweets.

L'Olandese Volante 27

V. S. Gallo 44r

🚍 Buses 1, 6 and 17

Open: daily 0830–1300, 1430–2000, closed Mon am

'The Flying Dutchman' offers a taste of the Low Countries in the heart of Renaissance Florence. As you'd expect, there's a huge array of Dutch cheeses and crackers, also spicy bread (*speculoos*), cinnamon toffee and multi-flavoured chocolate sweets.

Robiglio 28

V. dei Servi 112r

🚍 Bus C

Open: Mon–Sat 0800–2000

One of Florence's best-known confectioners, the name Robiglio has become synonymous with quality. Apart from chocolates, there are mouth-watering displays of delicate Florentine pastries (the savoury croissants are particularly delectable), cakes, tarts and biscuits.

Conad 29

V. dei Servi 56r

🚍 Buses 14 and 23

Open: daily 0800–2000

One of the few supermarkets in the city centre.

Osteria dell' Ortelano 30

V. degli Alfani 91

🚍 Buses 1, 6 and 17

Open: daily 0800–1400, 1630–2000

Local delicatessen where you can shop for Tuscan salamis and cheeses. They also sell Chianti in the traditional straw flasks.

I Sapori dei Chianti 31

V. dei Servi 10r

🚍 Buses 14 and 23

Open: daily 1000–1300, 1500–2000

The rack of bottles by the door is the perfect advertisement for this excellent wine shop, specialising in Chianti, but with a good selection of wines from the regions, Barolo and Barbaresco for example.

Vini 32

V. degli Alfani 76r

🚍 Bus C

Open: daily 1000–1400, 1630–2000

This tiny wine shop specialises in classic Tuscan labels such as Marchese Antinori. They also sell *Rocca di Montegrosso* virgin olive oil and gift boxes of white cream truffles.

▲ Dulcis

In the suburbs

For the more adventurous . . .

The following is a selection of the better known out-of-town eateries, most with fairly convenient locations and public transport links.

• **Burde** *V. Pistoiese 6r; ✆ 055 317206;* 🚍 *bus 35; open: Mon–Sat 1100–1500; reservations recommended; all credit cards accepted; Tuscan;* ❷❷. On the road to the airport, Burde is a suburban *fiaschetteria* open for lunches only. There are extensive seating areas at the back of the shop. The food is unpretentious but zestful and flavoursome. *Crostini, ribollita*, pasta dishes and delicious meat stews are at the forefront of a resolutely Tuscan menu. Don't eat more than a light breakfast beforehand as the portions are enormous!

• **Di' Sordo** *V. Vicenzo Gioberti 170–2r; ✆ 055 245634;* 🚍 *buses 6 and 14; open: Mon–Sat 1200–1430, 1900–2300; reservations recommended; all credit cards accepted; Tuscan-Italian;* ❷❷. A relative newcomer, this trattoria east of Santa Croce is friendly, relaxed and refreshingly down to

▲ *Crostini*

earth. You can sit indoors or at a table on the pavement. Open your account with a fresh salad or carpaccio and follow with one of the well-cooked pasta dishes. The main courses feature not only the predictable line-up of grilled meats but wholesome Tuscan stews and fish. Limited wine list.

• **La Focaccia** *Vle Corsica 31r; ✆ 055 350663;* 🚍 *bus 23; open: Mon–Sat ; reservations essential; all credit cards accepted; Tuscan;* ❷❷–❷❷❷. The young couple who started the business only a few years ago are now beginning to find their feet. By cooking for only a few people at once (there's room for only a few tables), David and Barbara can focus on their creative bent, which is to combine Tuscan standards such as *ribollita* or *minestra di faro* with the frankly exotic – where else in Florence would you find kangaroo on the menu? The tuna mousse with pearl barley is an out-and-out winner.

• **Le Piramidi** *V. di Rosano 198, Bagno a Ripoli; ✆ 055 6519000;* 🚍 *buses 31, 32 and 33; open: daily 1200–1430, 1900–2230; reservations recommended; all credit cards accepted; Tuscan-Italian;* ❷❷. Once part of the rural hinterland of Florence, Bagno a Ripoli is now classed as a suburb, though it has retained some of its charm. This local serves excellent value Tuscan dishes. To start, try the cold sliced meats or the *sformati di* *verdure*, a kind of vegetable soufflé. Pasta is served simply with olives and tomatoes or *rucola* (rocket). Main courses include tureen of white meats or *bistecca alla fiorentina*, made with beef from the Chianina cows and cooked to perfection. Selection of Chianti and other Tuscan wines.

• **Trattoria da Mamma Elissa** *V. Carlo d' Angiò 60–2; ✆ 055 6801370; 🚍 bus 8; open: daily 1200–1430, 1900–2230; reservations essential; all credit cards accepted; Tuscan; ❶❶*. At Mama Elissa's you can be sure of at least one thing: the fish arrives fresh on the table every day. It's worth leaving the confines of the city for the *cacciucco livornese* alone. This hot and spicy fish soup, made with *casalingo* bread, tomatoes, chilli peppers and shellfish – so thick that it's almost a stew – is found all too rarely on Tuscan tables nowadays. The chef uses similar ingredients as the basis for his *pièce de résistance*, paella. Ask the waiter for advice about which of the white wines is best suited to your meal.

• **Trattoria di' Sor Paolo** *V. Cassia per Firenze 38–40; ✆ 055 828402; 🚍 buses 22 and 23; open: dinner Thu–Sun; lunch Sat–Sun; reservations essential; all credit cards accepted; Tuscan; ❶–❶❶*. This delightful trattoria is on the main Florence–Siena road. Don't set out unless you're as enthusiastic about Tuscan food and its traditions as Mario your host. Follow his advice or

perhaps start with the liver pâté on toasted bread, followed by pasta ribbons in a wild boar sauce. The main courses of grilled meats (including pork, beef and kid) are cooked as they should be, *alla brace* (over an open fire). Treat yourself to one of the homemade desserts, assuming you still have room.

• **La Vecchia Cucina** *Vle Edmondo de Amicis 1r; ✆ 055 660143; 🚍 buses 3, 6 and 20; open: daily 1200–1430, 1900–2300; reservations recommended; all credit cards accepted; Tuscan-Italian; ❶❶*. The ambitious owner of this stylish *ristorante*, located beyond the stadium, has produced not one but four menus: pasta, meat, fish and vegetarian. The emphasis here is on freshness, with vegetables available strictly according to season and homemade pasta. Wine enthusiasts will also appreciate a list which encompasses all the great Italian regions (including, of course, Tuscany).

• **Vittoria** *V. della Fonderia 52r; ✆ 055 225657; 🚍 bus 6; open: daily 1200–1430, 1900–2230; reservations recommended; all credit cards accepted; Tuscan; ❶❶–❶❶❶*. A trattoria with a growing reputation for its fish dishes – shellfish especially. Try the shrimps scented with citrus to start or the risotto made with crab and other crustaceans. The grilled fish platter makes an excellent main course. The waiter is on hand to help you choose your white wines.

Try the shrimps scented with citrus to start or the risotto made with crab and other crustaceans.

Piazza della Repubblica

Leading from Via del Corso, Florence's main street, are labyrinthine back streets, crammed with restaurants and trattorias of every size and description. By contrast, the large open space of the Piazza della Repubblica attracts crowds of people-watchers, sunning themselves on the café terraces.

PIAZZA DELLA REPUBBLICA
Restaurants

Bierreria Centrale ❶

Pza dei Cimatori 1/2r	
✆ 055 211915	
🚍 Bus A	
Open: Mon–Sat 1200–1600, 1900–2400	
Reservations essential	
All credit cards accepted	
Bavarian-Italian	
€€	

This lovely, old saloon was founded in 1898 and retains its dark wooden benches and tables. It's a favourite with locals and tourists alike and if you want lunch, it's a good idea to come early. Bierreria is famous for its Bavarian specialities: roebuck, shin of pork with sauerkraut, smoked goose breast, and so on. However, don't despair if you're not over-enamoured of meat, there are also vegetarian dishes including omelettes, artichokes served with parmesan cheese, couscous, pasta, and so on. Naturally, this is also a mecca for beer connoisseurs – the choice of non-filtered draught beers includes Warsteiner Light, Peroni double malt and Abbé de Bonne Esperance.

The Bristol ❷

Hotel Helvetia and Bristol, V. dei Pescioni 2	
✆ 055 287814	
🚍 Bus A	
Open: daily 1200–1500, 1900–2300	
Reservations recommended	
All credit cards accepted	
Italian	
€€€	

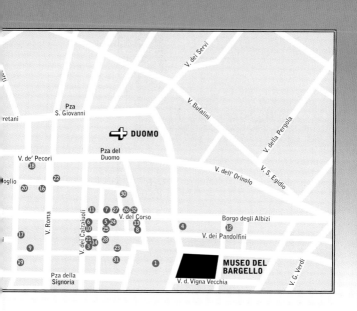

Ristorante il Paiolo

Diners at this famous hotel have included the composer Igor Stravinsky, the artist Giorgio de Chirico, film star Gary Cooper, poet Gabriele d' Annunzio, playwright Luigi Pirandello and nuclear physicist Enrico Fermi. The Bristol is also known for its award-winning décor – the shell chandeliers in the restaurant were lifted from the villa of an eccentric aristocrat on the island of Capri. The chef has remained loyal to Tuscan culinary traditions, so you can look forward to *fettunta* (toast with garlic and oil), pasta with beans and breast of chicken with spinach salad. He really goes to town with the desserts – difficult to choose between chocolate mousse with dried figs, sliced fresh fruit with honey ice cream, tiramisu (sponge cake with mascarpone, coffee and chocolate) and warm pear-filled puff pastry with spices and custard. In line with contemporary medical advice all meals are prepared with low-fat content. If you haven't time to dine here, at least call in for tea (*daily 1400–1900*) or an aperitif in the hotel's sumptuous **Winter Garden.**

I Cinque Amici

V. dei Cimatori 30r	
✆ 055 23 96672	
🚍 Bus A	
Open: daily 1200–1430, 1900–2300	
Reservations recommended	
All credit cards accepted	
Tuscan	
❷ ❷	

Ideally situated between the Duomo and the Palazzo Vecchio, this modern restaurant compensates for its lack of atmosphere by producing some highly creditable Tuscan dishes: *pappardelle alla lepre* (pasta ribbons in a hare sauce), *spezzatino con piselli* (meat stew with peas) and an *antipasto* of cold cuts.

Da Gastone

V. del Proconsolo 55r	
✆ 055 294361	
🚍 Bus 15	
Open: Mon–Fri	
Reservations not allowed	
Tuscan	
❻ – ❻❻	

This restaurant has a nickname – 'alle mossacce', Tuscan dialect for a rude gesture! Lingering is not encouraged and if you enjoy bustle, so much the better. The food, including the usual range of typical Florentine dishes, is excellent, as is the location between the Duomo and the Bargello.

Nanchino ❺

V. dei Cerchi 36–40r	
✆ 055 213142	
🚍 Buses 14, 23 and A	
Open: daily 1200–1500, 1900–2400	
Reservations recommended	
All credit cards accepted	
Chinese	
❻❻	

One of the leading Chinese restaurants in Florence, Nanchino offers a large choice of beef, chicken, shellfish and vegetable dishes. The ambience here is calm and relaxed, the service courteous and attentive, while the no smoking regulation is a definite plus.

Paoli ❻

V. dei Tavolini 12r	
✆ 055 216215	
🚍 Bus A	
Open: Wed–Mon 1200–1430, 1900–2230	
Reservations recommended	
💳 American Express	
Tuscan-Italian	
❻❻	

Right in the heart of Renaissance Florence, this rather formal restaurant celebrates the city's historic pedigree with a marvellous pastiche of a vaulted medieval hall, complete with embossed coats of arms and painted ceilings. Well suited to a leisurely lunch, with a choice of several set menus as well as à la carte.

Il Paiolo **7**

V. del Corso 42r	
✆ 055 215019	
🚍 Buses 14 and 23	
Open: Mon–Sat 1200–1500, 1900–2300	
Reservations unnecessary	
🌐 American Express	
Tuscan-Italian	
❻❻	

This cosy trattoria is within walking distance of the Duomo. Multilingual waiters will take you through the menu, which focuses on typical Tuscan dishes such as *costoletta di maiale alla fiorentina* (pork cutlet). There's a tourist menu if you prefer and a more expensive all-inclusive option for vegetarians.

Pennello **8**

V. Dante Alighieri 4r	
✆ 055 294848	
🚍 Bus A	
Open: Tue–Sun 1200–1500, 1900–2200, closed Sun evening	
Reservations recommended	
All credit cards accepted	
Italian	
❻❻	

This *osteria* dates back to the 16th century when it was founded by the painter, Mariotto Albertinelli. It was frequented by such illustrious artists as Benvenuto Cellini, Andrea Del Sarto and Michelangelo, while much earlier it was the home of the poet Dante. Today the interior has been modernised but there are still reminders of the past, exposed brick vaulting, decorated capitals, and so on. Pennello is famous for its wonderful salad bar – every day the chef prepares more than 20 bowls, using only the freshest produce. Otherwise it's typical Tuscan cuisine with the celebrated *bistecca alla fiorentina* to the fore.

▲ The Bristol's Winter Garden

PIAZZA DELLA REPUBBLICA
Bars, cafés and pubs

Antico Café de Ritti ❾

V. dei Lamberti 9r

☎ 055 2912583

🚌 Bus A

Open: Mon–Sat 0700–2100

€

Ritti literally means 'on your feet', and alludes to the tradition of eating and drinking at the counter. There's seating here too, of course, and Ritti makes an excellent stop for breakfast or light lunch, when you can eat either *antipasti* or single course dishes such as curried prawns or pasta with chickpeas. The food is laid out on trays, making it easy to point if you don't know Italian. The hot doughnuts arrive at 1630 every day and the bar serves Bitburger and Bass beers on draught.

Cantinetta dei Verrazzano ❿

V. dei Tavolini

☎ 055 268590

🚌 Bus A

Open: Mon–Sat

€–€€

This wine bar is an outlet for Chianti Classico wines from the Verrazzano estate near Greve. You can also buy snacks including scrumptious bread,

freshly baked in the oven, salami, *focaccia* (a kind of pizza) and Tuscan biscuits.

Chiaroscuro ⓫

V. del Corso 36r

☎ 055 214247

🚌 Bus A

Open: Mon–Sat 0730–2030

€

This friendly café in the heart of downtown Florence is noted for its selection of coffees from all over the globe (available for sale). You can take a light lunch or, in the evenings, an aperitif or glass of wine with a snack.

Enoteca de' Giraldi ⓬

V. de' Giraldi 4r

☎ 055 213881

🚌 Bus A

Open: Mon–Sat 1100–0100

€€

Attractively situated in the old shops of the Palazzo Borghese, this large wine bar with excellent selections of wines from Tuscany and central Italy – note the Brunello di Montalcino, for example – also has a good food counter with a choice of hot soups, carpaccio,

salads, *crostini*, salami, cheeses and sugary desserts from the Robiglio patisserie. For wine connoisseurs there are tastings in English on Wednesdays at 1830. The price includes sampling four wines, *crostini* and cheeses as well as expert advice.

▲ Giubbe Rosse

Festival del Gelato 🔞

V. del Corso 75r
✐ None available
🚍 Bus A
Open: daily 1000–2300
€

Don't allow the glaring purple lights, loud pop music and videos to put you off, as this café sells an astonishing variety of ice creams, the more unusual include tiramisu, Ferrero Rocher, profiteroles and Mars bar.

Fiaschetteria 'i Fratellinni' 🔞

V. dei Cimatori 38r
✐ None available
🚍 Bus A
Open: Mon–Sat
€

No wonder it's a tight squeeze here – this famous bar is the smallest in town. As the name implies, brothers have run the place ever since it first opened in 1875. You can't sit down – there just isn't enough room, but it's great fun to stand at the bar and sample from the wide choice of wines on offer. If you fancy a bite to eat, go for the *crostini*.

Giacosa 🔞

V. Tournabouni, corner of V. della Spada
✐ 055 244733
🚍 Buses 6, 11, 36 and 37
Open: Mon–Sat 0730–2030
€

Owned by the same family as Rivoire on Piazza della Signoria, this smaller café is run

on similar lines with bustling, formally attired waiters and tempting window displays. Open for breakfast and sells sandwiches, pastries, cakes, biscuits and wines.

Gilli

V. Roma 1/8	
✆ 055 213896	
🚍 Bus A	
Open: Wed–Mon 0800–2200	
❻❻	

Founded in the 18th century as a humble pastry shop, Gilli later went up-market. Today the atmosphere is period while the décor verges on the luxurious, with marble counters, wood-panelled walls and white-painted stucco arches. Suave eagle-eyed waiters are forever in attendance and on the look out for tips. To accompany your coffee, there's a choice of American breakfast, standard pasta dishes and grills and mouth-watering desserts – the tiramisu is recommended.

Giubbe Rosse

Pza della Repubblica 13–14r	
✆ 055 212280	
🚍 Bus A	
Open: daily 0700–0130	
❻	

This well-known literary café, very grand and formal, serves American breakfasts between 0800 and 1100 (bacon and eggs, toast, brioche, coffee) as well as nourishing light lunches, for example, spaghetti with eggs, cheese and bacon, *rucola* salad, and so on.

Leonardo

V. de' Pecori 5r	
✆ 055 284446	
🚍 Buses 22, 36 and 37	
Open: Sun–Fri 1145–1445, 1845–2145	
❻	

Self-service restaurant, right in the centre of town, selling good-value *casalinga* Tuscan cuisine.

The Old Stove

V. Pellicceria 24r	
✆ None available	
🚍 Bus A	
Open: Tue–Fri 1200–0230, Sat–Mon 1500–0230	
❻	

The smallest Irish bar in the city, with unreliable waitress service and noisy music, still draws the crowds. Few obvious Celtic influences apart from the Guinness.

Paszkowski

Pza della Republica 35r	
✆ 055 217438	
🚍 Bus A	
Open: daily 0800–2200	
❻	

Café redolent of old-style elegance, with formal service and terrace seating overlooking the square. Best suited to morning coffee or afternoon tea.

Perché No!

V. dei Tavolini 19r	
✆ 055 2398969	
🚍 Bus A	

Open: Wed–Mon

❻

'Why not!' has been selling ice cream from its city centre location since 1939. Try the extra creamy *semifreddo* (frozen mousse) in flavours such as *zuppa inglese* (trifle) or one of their *sorbetti* (iced fruit and sugar).

Robiglio

V. Tosinghi 11r	
✆ 055 214501	
🚍 Bus A	
Open: daily 0730–2000	
❻	

One of Florence's best-known patisseries, Robiglio has become synonymous with quality. Apart from chocolates, this branch sells mouth-watering delicate Florentine pastries (the savoury croissants are particularly delectable), cakes, tarts and biscuits.

Tripe stall

Pzetta dei Cimatori	
✆ None available	
🚍 Bus A	
Open: Mon–Sat 0900–1430, 1700–1900	
❻	

The Florentine delicacy, *lampredotto* – hot, greasy tripe sandwiches, wrapped in thick paper – can be tried in Piazzetta dei Cimatori, on the corner of Via Calzaiuoli. Palmiro Pinzauti doles out his tripe without the usual trimmings of hot sauces or salads, but this doesn't seem to put the locals off.

PIAZZA DELLA REPUBBLICA
Shops, markets and picnic sites

Bakeries, confectioners and pasta shops

Dolci & Dolcezze ㉔

V. del Corso 41r

🚍 Bus A

Open: daily 0730–2000

Patisserie selling croissants, cream cakes and savoury pastries.

Sartoni ㉕

V. dei Cerchi 34r

🚍 Bus A

Open: daily 0800–2000

Centrally located baker's shop, sellling typically Tuscan salt-free bread and biscuits.

Delicatessens and grocers

La cultura dell' espresso ㉖

V. del Corso 36r

🚍 Bus A

Open: daily 1000–2000

This delightful coffee emporium on one of Florence's major thoroughfares has become something of a shrine for connoisseurs. Tastings are available and light lunches are served in the wine bar.

Grana ㉗

V. del Corso 11r

🚍 Bus A

Open: daily 0800–2000

A well-stocked supermarket with the usual range of groceries and soft and alcoholic drinks, also a delicatessen counter.

Mauro ㉘

V. dei Cerchi 16r

🚍 Bus A

Open: Tue–Sun 0730–1345, 1700–1930, closed Wed pm

Local fruiterers located on a picturesque medieval street, overlooked by a 13th-century watchtower. Mauro also sells preserves, soft drinks and flasks of Chianti wine.

Old England Stores ㉙

V. de' Vecchietti 28r

🚍 Bus A

Open: daily 1000–1330, 1600–1930

Old-fashioned emporium founded in the 19th century to sell traditional English foodstuffs to homesick travellers.

Pegna ㉚

V. dello Studio 26r

🚍 Bus A

Open: daily 0800–1330, 1530–2000

Established in 1860 and retaining its quaint genteel atmosphere, this small supermarket by the Duomo is well stocked with a tempting selection of local products.

Wines and oils

Bizzarri ㉛

V. Condotta 32

🚍 Bus A

Open: daily 1000–1430, 1630–1930

An unusual store devoted to wine growing and the Tuscan kitchen.

La Galleria del Chianti ㉜

V. del Corso 41r

🚍 Bus A

Open: daily 1000–1430, 1630–2000

This little wine shop is full to bursting with the very best of Chianti Classico.

▲ Dolci & Dolcezze

Florentine sweetmeats and desserts

The blending of honey and sugar

Florentines have always had a sweet tooth. Honey satisfied them as a sweetener until they became acquainted with **sugar** towards the end of the 15th century, when it was imported from Madeira. Soon there was a craze for the stuff and no banquet was complete without its sugar fantasy. In 1600, Pietro Tacca spent four months modelling giant 'sugar statues' to adorn the banquet celebrating the wedding of Maria de' Medici to Henri IV of France, at an estimated cost of 1 700 gold florins.

Ordinary citizens still had to make do with **honey**, however, and most Tuscan desserts are humble affairs, traditionally made with left over bread. One of the most popular is **schiacciata**. *Schiacciata con l'uva* is, as the name suggests, made with black-grape jam. This delicious sweet makes its appearance in bakeries and cake shops during September and October, coinciding with the harvest. *Schiacciata alla fiorentina* is an orange or lemon sponge cake, flat and rectangular in appearance. You'll see it advertised in shop windows year round, but especially at carnival time. You'll also see *zuccotto* on dessert trolleys; a much lighter sponge, it's usually flavoured with chocolate, Cointreau or rum. *Panforte* is another traditional bread-based delicacy. It dates back to the 13th century and was originally made with honey and fruit. The name, meaning 'strong (i.e. sour) bread', referred to its tendency to go mouldy quickly. Honey is still an ingredient, though nowadays sugar is added.

Many Florentines start the day with a **cake**. A favourite is the *bombolone*, a doughnut filled with cream or custard. Look out for the sign 'Bombolone Caldo' with the time they're expected hot from the bakeries.

Tuscany is famous for its **biscuits**. The pick of the bunch is *cantuccini*, also known as *biscotti di Prato*. If you visit a traditional restaurant such as **I Latini** (*see page 60*), you'll be offered these circular, almond-flavoured confections after your dessert, together with the delectable sweet wine known as Vin Santo. As *cantuccini* can be hard on the teeth, the custom is to dunk them in the wine.

▲ *Cantuccini*

Every bakery worth its salt sells *cenci*, another sweetmeat associated with Shrovetide, made with flour and butter, a few drops of marsala wine and a generous topping of vanilla icing sugar – the name suggests snippets or clippings. *Cavallucci*, like many Tuscan biscuits are Sienese in origin. Resembling lumps of bread dough, they're spicy and flavoured with honey, candied orange peel and walnuts; like *cantuccini*, they taste even better when dunked in Vin Santo.

Almonds have been an important ingredient in biscuits and cakes since they first made their appearance in cookbooks, together with marzipan in the 15th century. *Ricciarelli* are almond biscuits, closely associated with Christmas; during Lent the shelves fill with boxes of *quaresimali*, chocolate biscuits cut into the shape of letters of the alphabet and a favourite with children.

• **La Boutique dei Dolci** *V. Giovanni Fabroni 18r;* ☺ *bus 4; open: daily 0830–2030.* The latest fashion in desserts are available here, including themed cakes and biscuit boxes.

• **Dolci & Dolcezze** *Pza Beccaria 8r;* ☺ *buses 8, 12, 31 and 32; open: Tue–Sun 0830–2030.* Master pastry chef, Giulio Corti, is renowned for his sweets, all made with the freshest ingredients. This is the place to come for seasonal specialities.

• **Minni** *V. Antonio Giacomini 16;* ☺ *buses 10, 11, 17 and 20;* *open: daily 0830–2000.* Hot *bomboloni* are delivered daily at 1700 here. Also look out for *brutti ma buoni* ('ugly but good'), little biscuits made with hazelnuts and egg white.

> **Look out for 'brutti ma buoni' ('ugly but good'), little biscuits made with hazelnuts and egg white.**

• **Rivoire** *Pza della Signoria;* ∅ *055 214412;* ☺ *bus A; open: Tue–Sun 0800–2400;* ●●●. Best known for its views – tables overlooking the Palazzo Vecchio are at a premium, so if you see one, grab it – Rivoire is an elegant *pasticceria* famous for its chocolate. Sandwiches and a range of mouth-watering desserts are also available, but at a price. Bear in mind that you pay extra if you sit outside.

Food etiquette and culture

WHERE TO EAT

Deciding whether to eat in a *ristorante* or a trattoria is largely a matter of how much you want to pay and the degree of formality you're looking for. Generally speaking, **trattorias** are less expensive, have a more relaxed ambience, and only rarely add a cover charge. As for the quality of the food, paying more doesn't necessarily mean eating better – indeed if you're a fan of Tuscan *cucina casalinga* (home cooking), a trattoria is often superior. For light lunches, the neighbourhood café is a good bet – remember that it's a little more expensive to sit at a table than to stand at the counter.

There are four different types of wine bar. All serve food of some kind as Italians rarely drink on an empty stomach. While a meal in an *enoteca* may rival a good restaurant in terms of quality, most customers are wine enthusiasts. *Enoteche* are major outlets for Chianti Classico and other regional wines which you can order by the glass. The traditional wine shop or tavern (now sadly on the decline) has a variety of names: *mescita*, *fiaschetteria* (a reminder of the days when all Chianti came in straw-covered flasks), or *vinaio*. Usually it's standing room only, with one or two tables at most. As well as wine you can order

filled rolls and appetisers (*crostini*, salami, and so on). It's here that you'll see the older generation whiling away the afternoon with a newspaper or exchanging gossip over a glass of wine.

Most **pizzerias** serve pasta and meat dishes as well. If you want your pizza cooked in the traditional way (*forno a legna*), you may have to wait until the wood-fuelled oven is lit in the evening. Local bakeries and some delicatessens sell pizza slices (*pizza a taglio*) and *calzone*, a savoury turnover made with pizza dough. Coarse, unsalted Tuscan bread (*casalingo*), fresh from the oven, is used to make rolls and sandwiches in the city's bakeries. Another useful outlet is the pastry shop *pasticceria*, where you can fill up on cakes and savouries.

Bars also serve food (often quite good) and let's not forget the humble *trippaio*, or tripe stall, still very popular with Florentines.

If you're a **vegetarian**, the choice is limited as there are hardly any designated vegetarian restaurants in Florence. That said, there'll always be something on the menu to try – many soups, salads and pasta dishes are meat free. A word of warning: if you order vegetable soup, check that it's been cooked using vegetable stock or *brodo vegetariano*.

WHEN TO EAT

Most Italians make do with a light **breakfast**, comprising a cake or *brioche* (a bun filled with custard or jam) and a cappuccino. Sunday brunch is a foreign import which is beginning to catch on – you'll also see American and English breakfasts advertised here and there. Except on Sundays, you won't have a problem finding a table for **lunch** as most office workers are content with a sandwich. There's usually a fixed price menu *menù turistico*, if you don't want to order à la carte.

In the **evenings** many Florentines dine early – some trattorias are already busy by eight. Some of the more popular eateries work on the basis of two sittings, 1930 and 2130, although this isn't official. Kitchens close around 2230 but there's no need to hurry your meal as most restaurants don't close before midnight.

Booking is essential in Florence (even in winter) if you want to be sure of eating in the restaurant or trattoria of your choice. Even if you have booked you may have to wait in line. Some trattorias won't accept advance bookings, so the best policy is to arrive early (around 1900) or much later (after 2100).

HOW TO ORDER

It's useful to bear in mind that if you're eating in a restaurant or trattoria, ordering only one course is frowned on, so if you don't want to linger over a meal choose an alternative.

An Italian menu is divided into at least four sections.

Antipasti are appetisers which you can skip if you wish. *Primi* are first courses or starters, usually pasta dishes, or more commonly in Florence, nourishing bread based soups. Main courses are called *secondi*. In Italy, vegetables are often listed separately as *contorni* or you might prefer a salad (*insalata*). You might finish with a *dolce* (dessert) or *formaggio* (cheese). Coffee, always served at the end of the meal, is invariably black *espresso*. Many Italians order a *digestif* (an Amaro or other liqueur), while a popular Florentine alternative is *cantuccini* (almond biscuits) dunked in a glass of the sweet wine known as Vin Santo.

HOW TO PAY

When paying, make sure you receive a printed and itemised receipt (*un ricevuto*), anything else is illegal. In an average restaurant, taxes and service will be included as well as the *coperto*, a nominal charge, intended to cover bread and payable per person.

▲ Waiter at Bibò

Menu decoder

COOKING METHODS
affumicato – smoked
arrosto – roasted
fatto in casa – homemade
al forno – cooked in an oven
forno a legna – cooked in a
    wood-fired oven
fritto – fried
griglia – grilled
ripieno – stuffed

DRESSINGS
aceto – vinegar
olio di oliva – olive oil
panna – cream
pepe – pepper
sale – salt
salsa – sauce
senape – mustard; also *mostarda*

BREADS
focaccia – a kind of flat, unsalted
    Tuscan bread, usually
    seasoned with olive oil
pane – generic name for bread –
    in Florence it will be thick
    textured, rather coarse and
    unsalted; it's often referred to
    as *casalingo*

panini – bread rolls
pizza a taglio – pizza slice

APPETISERS (*Antipasti*)
affettati misti – cold meat slices,
    including Tuscan ham, salami,
    boar sausage
antipasti misto – a selection of
    appetisers which might consist
    of a combination of Tuscan
    ham, salami, *mortadella*
    (salted pork), raw vegetables,
    large juicy black or green
    olives, marinated mushrooms,
    tomatoes
bruschetta – slices of unsalted
    Tuscan bread, toasted and
    rubbed with a clove of garlic,
    with a drizzle of olive oil;
    often served with tomatoes
    dressed with basil or white
    beans
crostini – slices of unsalted
    Tuscan bread smeared
    generously with veal or
    chicken liver pâté
finocchiona – salami flavoured
    with fennel seeds

olive – olives
prosciutto crudo –
    salted cured ham

FIRST COURSE
(*Primi (piatti)*)
acquacotta – a thick
nourishing soup made
with cabbage, chard
and vegetables
brodo – broth
cecina – flat crispy
bread made from
chickpea flour

▲ *Crostini*

fettuccine – long narrow ribbons of egg pasta

frittata – a kind of omlette

gnocchi – dumplings, usually served with a sauce

minestra – usually implies a vegetable soup made with black cabbage, beans, onion, tomatoes and carrots

pappa al pomodoro – tomato mush made with ripe tomatoes and stale bread, left in a saucepan to turn into a pulp, then seasoned with basil

pappardelle – a kind of pasta

panzanella – a salad made with tomatoes, onions and crumbled Tuscan bread

passato – puréed soup

pasta e fagioli – pasta and white Tuscan beans

ribollita – a thick vegetable broth, containing Tuscan black cabbage and slices of soaked, unsalted bread

tortelli – stuffed pasta

zuppa di verdura – vegetable soup

FISH AND SEAFOOD

acciughe – anchovies

aragosta – lobster

baccalà – dried salted cod

banchetti – little fish like whitebait

calamari – squid

cappe sante – scallops

coda di rospo – monkfish tails

cozze – mussels

fritto misto – mixed fried fish

gamberetti – shrimps

gamberi – prawns

granchio – crab

insalata di mare – seafood salad

merluzzo – cod

ostriche – oysters

pesce – generic word for fish

pesce spada – swordfish

polpo – octopus

rospo – monkfish

San Pietro – John Dory

sarde (sardine) – sardines

spigola (branzino) – sea bass

sogliola – sole, *alla griglia* (grilled), *alla mugnaia* (in butter)

tonno – tuna

trota – trout

vongole – clams

MEAT, POULTRY AND GAME

agnello – lamb

anatra – duck

arrosto mista – mixed roast meats, including lamb, pork, sausage and chicken liver

bistecca – beefsteak

bressaola – raw dried pork served in thin slices

caccia – generic term for game

carpaccio – raw beef served in thin slices

capretto – kid

cervo – venison

cinghiale – wild boar, now mostly found in pâtés and salami

coniglio – rabbit, very common, especially stewed with olives

cotoletta – chop

fagiano – pheasant

fegato – liver

filetto – fillet

lepre – hare

maiale – pork

manzo – beef

ossobuco – stew made with knuckle of veal in tomato sauce

pancetta – a kind of bacon

prosciutto – ham

piccione – pigeon, served either roasted or in pâté

pollo – chicken

porchetta – roast pork

rognone – kidney

salsicce – sausage

tacchino – turkey
trippa – tripe
vitello –veal

HERBS, PULSES AND VEGETABLES

aglio – garlic
asparagi – asparagus
capperi – capers
carciofi – artichokes
carote – carrots
cavolfiore – cauliflower
cavolo nero – a dark variety of
    cabbage
ceci – chickpeas
cetriolo – cucumber
cipolla – onion
contorni – generic term for
    vegetables
erbe – herbs
fagioli – white beans
fagiolini – green, string or French
    beans
faro – wheat, usually found in
    soup
fave – broad beans
funghi – mushrooms; *funghi
    porcini* are ceps; *funghi
    selvatici*, wild mushrooms
lattuga – lettuce
lenticchie – lentils

mandorle – almonds
melanzane – aubergine
patate – potatoes
peperoncino – chilli pepper
peperoni – peppers
pinoli – pinenuts
pinzimonio – selection of raw
    vegetables to be dipped in
    olive oil
piselli – peas
pomodoro – tomato
porri – leeks
rucola – rocket salad
tartufo – truffles
zucchini – courgettes

FRUIT

albicocche – apricots
ananas – pineapple
arance – oranges
banane – bananas
ciliege – cherries
cocomero – watermelon
datteri – dates
fichi – figs
fragole – strawberries
lamponi – raspberries
limone – lemons
macedonia di frutta – fruit salad
mele – apples
melone – melons

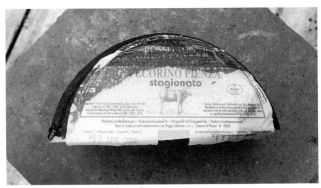

▲ Pecorino

more – blackberries
pere – pears
pesche – peaches
pompelmo – grapefruit
uva – grapes

DESSERTS AND CHEESE

amaretti – macaroons
brioche – (pronounced as in French) bun or pastry made with sweet yeast dough and filled with cream, custard or jam
brutti e buoni – biscuits made of hazelnuts and egg white
cantuccini – biscuits traditionally dunked in Vin Santo; also *biscotti di Prato*
castagnaccio – chestnut flour cake
cavallucci – spice biscuits with honey, nuts and candied orange peel
cenci – fritters, with a few drops of marsala or liqueur as well as a coating of icing sugar
gelato – ice cream
granita – flavoured ice
mandorlata – almond brittle
necci – pancakes served with ricotta and preserves
ossi di morto – biscuits with almond and egg white
panforte – dense cake, made with almonds, honey and dried fruit
pecorino – traditional Tuscan sheeps' milk cheese
ricciarelli – almond biscuits
schiacciata con l'uva – bread-based pastry with grape jam
tiramisu – sponge, mascarpone, coffee and chocolate
torta – tart or cake
zabaglione – hot whipped egg and marsala
zuccotto – a dome shaped Madeira cake with whipped cream, nuts and chocolate chips
zuppa inglese – trifle

DRINKS

acqua (minerale) – (mineral) water; *gassata* – sparkling, *senza gas* – still
una bicchiere – a glass of wine
birra – beer; *birra alla spina* – draught beer; sizes are usually *piccola* (small), *media* (medium) and *grande* (large)
bottiglia – bottle
caffè – coffee; cappuccino (coffee with milk froth), *corretto* (with a dash of grappa), *caffè latte* (a milky cappuccino)
cioccolata – hot chocolate
latte – milk; *uno frullato* is a milkshake
succo di frutta – fruit juice; freshly squeezed – *una spremuta*
tè – tea

WINES

vino (rosso, bianco, rosato) – wine (red, white, rosé); dry is *secco*
Brunello di Montalcino – noted red Chianti wine made from the Sangiovese grape
Chianti – red wine from the Chianti region of Tuscany, made predominantly from the Sangiovese grape
Nobile di Montepulciano – one of the finest Tuscan reds, made with the Sangiovese grape
Trebbiano – the most common Tuscan white wine
Vernaccia di San Gimignano – among the best of the Tuscan whites
Vin Santo – yellowish dessert wine, made with leftover Trebbiano or (better) Malvasia grapes

Recipes

Acquacotta

Serves 4

INGREDIENTS

8 slices stale bread
225g canned tomatoes
1 clove garlic
1 dried chilli, crushed
1 stick celery, finely chopped
1 carrot, sliced
200g broad beans
300g peas
300g chard
2 onions finely chopped
4 tbsp extra virgin olive oil
salt
black pepper
4 eggs
60g grated parmesan cheese*
1 litre boiling water

ACQUACOTTA

trattoria tipica toscana

Via dei Pilastri, 51 r.
FIRENZE
Telef. 242.907

CHIUSO LA
DOMENICA

First clean the chard and trim the leaves. Heat the oil in a large pot (preferably made of terracotta). Gently fry the onion, peas, beans, carrots, celery and chilli on a medium heat until softened. Add the chard, tomatoes and a little water and simmer for 15 minutes. Then add the rest of the water and salt to taste and boil slowly for 40 minutes.

In a basin beat the eggs, then add the cheese, salt and pepper, Toast the bread on both sides and rub with the garlic clove. Place two slices of toast in each soup bowl and cover with the beaten egg

mixture. Pour the soup over the toast and stir well. Serve at once.

* To make the dish even more authentic, use Tuscan pecorino cheese rather than parmesan.

Zuccotto

Serves 4

INGREDIENTS

For the sponge:

4 eggs, separated

150g icing sugar

75g plain flour

75g cornflour

grated rind ½ lemon

For the filling:

2 tbsp brandy or rum

2 tbsp sweet liqueur (eg, Cointreau)

75g cooking chocolate

120g grated plain chocolate

½ litre fresh cream

50g icing sugar

30g blanched almonds

50g candied orange and lemon peel, chopped finely

To make the sponge, beat the egg yolks and sugar in a bowl until the mixture is light and frothy. In a separate bowl, whisk the egg whites until firm, then fold into the yolks. Slowly add the flours, stirring continually to prevent lumps. Grease and lightly flour a deep cake tin, then pour in the sponge mixture. Bake at Mark 4 (180°C, 350°F) for about 45 minutes. When the sponge is cooked, turn on to a rack and allow to cool.

Cut the sponge horizontally into slices 1cm thick, then into strips. Sprinkle with the brandy and liqueur. Line a mould or basin with buttered waxed paper, then place the sponge strips across the bottom and round the sides.

To make the filling, toast the almonds and chop roughly. Mix together half the grated chocolate, the almonds, the candied peel, the sugar and half of the cream. Melt the cooking chocolate in a double saucepan, allowing it to cool a little, then add the rest of the cream, stirring well. Pour the melted chocolate on to the sponge, spooning it carefully up the sides. Fill the centre of the sponge with the almond and candied peel mixture. Place the remaining sponge slices on top and then cover the bowl with tin foil and refrigerate for two hours. Turn on to a plate and sprinkle with grated chocolate and icing sugar.

Published by Thomas Cook Publishing
Thomas Cook Holdings Ltd
PO Box 227
Thorpe Wood
Peterborough PE3 6PU
United Kingdom

Telephone: 01733 503571
Email: books@thomascook.com

ISBN 1 841570 87 7

Distributed in the United States of
America by the Globe Pequot Press,
PO Box 480, Guilford, Connecticut
06437, USA

Publisher: Donald Greig
Commissioning Editor: Deborah Parker
Map Editor: Bernard Horton

Project management: Dial House
    Publishing
Series Editor: Christopher Catling
Copy Editor: Lucy Thomson
Proofreader: Lucy Thomson

Series and cover design: WhiteLight
Cover artwork: WhiteLight and
    Kaarin Wall
Text layout: SJM Design Consultancy,
    Dial House Publishing
Maps prepared by Polly Senior
    Cartography

Repro and image setting: PDQ Digital
    Media Solutions Ltd
Printed and bound in Italy by
    Eurografica SpA

Written and researched by: Chris and
    Melanie Rice

We would like to thank John Heseltine for
the photographs used in this book, to
whom the copyright belongs, with the
exception of the following:

Boscolo Hotels: (page 50)
The Charming Hotels: (page 81)
Neil Setchfield: (pages 57, 94 and 95).